MIXED BLOODLINE

The story of a young, biracial boy overcoming racism,
growing up in the South during the 1930s Jim Crow era

Octavia Yvonne Webb

Peggy,

A woman of Great Strength
+ Character. God's got
a Blessing!

Love,
Octavia Yvonne Webb
Psalm 37:4

Octavia Yvonne Webb

THE COLOR OF HATE

*Do you ever wonder, what color is hate? Do you ever imagine its
origination and fate? Blinding and vivid is its density, harrowing and
heart-wrenching is its intensity. What colors make up this prism of
fright, paring brother against brother fighting deep into the night.
How it torments the integrity of humanity pushing sane men to lose
their sanity. Who can carry this boulder of burden as to and fro . . . it
throbs of hurt and pain from long ago? Its mass is as wide as it is tall.
Its destiny is to see all men fall. Who can pursue this demon within
with claws of injustice at freedom's end? Who can withstand this fury
of fire that drowns all hope of saintly desire . . . only through Him do I
know. He galloped high with one fatal blow. He took the sting from a
broken heart and replaced it with love to heal a vital part. A part of
our being which color cannot reach and boastful pride cannot teach.*

*No weapon formed against man, nor tempting spices savored
deliciously in a bowl can tear or pierce the born-again soul.* --- Yvonne
Webb © 1995

contents

This book is written to give glory and honor to my Savior Jesus Christ and is dedicated to the memory of my father, James Leon Ivnes, for the legacy of integrity of work ethic, perseverance, and endurance despite unjustified obstacles and for a spirit of resiliency he left for our family to cherish.

Introduction

G ROWING UP AS A youngster, I was always amazed at the physical strength of my father. Like most Daddy's girls, I was amazed with him and his ability to do just about anything humanly possible. However, the one thing that Dad could not handle well was being biracial, and he struggled to identify who he was in a racially separated world. Even in the midst of all the chaos surrounding social injustice in the world at that particular time and much like today, Dad's objective was to overcome these obstacles and move forward to achieve self-worth.

The stories of his early life journey outlined in the following chapters only touch the surface of hardship, emotional hurt, and physical pain he endured. More than anything else, the legacy my dad passed along to me also revealed that perseverance and tenacity is a critical requirement to overcome the obstacles he faced.

During my adolescent years, I was not acutely aware of most of the harshness of racism particularly because of my parents' determination to protect me and my siblings. The humiliation and injustices my parents lived through, growing up in the South were common practice to them, but they were determined to protect us from this experience. My dad intentionally instilled in me and my siblings that hard work determined a person's character.

It was only as a young adult after leaving home and venturing out on my own that I realized what it felt like to be Black. I started to understand why Dad was determined to protect his children from what he experienced. He knew firsthand what it felt like to experience the emotional damage of years of oppression and live under substandard conditions. I empathized with the struggles Dad had experienced growing up. Observing how hard it was for him to push through these obstacles was sometimes overwhelming, but I never wanted to accept the hopelessness!

Dad believed if he worked hard enough at learning a skill, it would give him a chance to become successful and allow him a way to survive in a world of inferiority and hatred. For the most part, he accomplished that objective. He owned his own successful construction company without ever learning to read or write properly. He could only write his name. I watched him practice for sometimes hours trying to make his signature look legible. He tried to learn how to read, but he could not overcome and make significant—this was due largely, I believe, to a traumatic event he experienced as a child.

Segregation laws were strongly enforced in the education system while he was growing up. The systemic racist educational system of Jim Crow fueled ignorance against Black people, which was particularly intensified toward a person of mixed race. The end result of all of the injustice surrounding Dad obtaining an education was that it did not allow him to attend a White school while curiosity and social awkwardness stood in the way of his attending a Black school. His lack of education became the main obstacle that pounded an inferiority complex into his emotional stability. It pricked a hole at the very core of his self-identity and self-worth. This lingered around his perception of being a normal person and often led to his feelings of rejection and depression. The daily challenges he faced trying to be a provider for his family were overwhelming at times and most often culminated into frustration, anger, and rage.

However, Dad possessed such resiliency that through every circumstance, he would always come out on top of it all. Talk about receiving blessings even through hardship! I once heard a quote that broken crayons still color.

I learned great lessons from observing God's grace in my dad's life. Most importantly is the fact that I embraced faith in believing there was a higher power and presence in his life, undergirding, protecting, and allowing him to exist and survive in such a state of brokenness. It has been said the road of brokenness left unchecked can rob you of your life's blessing. I believe there is so much truth to this statement.

Dad did not recognize the blessings despite the brokenness he experienced, but I learned how to check those blind spots in my own personal life. I lived through watching my dad suffer through a lot during his lifetime. However, the grace and mercy extended to him by a loving and wise God still produced fruit in his life, which ultimately also extended fruit into my life. I have come full circle to acknowledge that Dad's life wasn't the only life broken—my life was broken too.

Many times, I witnessed my dad fly into a fit of rage and anger over petty issues. I never understood where all the anger came from until he began to share life events that happened to him growing up. Dad's determination to overcome living a life of oppression as outlined in the stories shared in this book prove as evidence that a person does not have to settle for living a defeated life. Rather, it serves to show others and hopefully readers of this book that unfortunate obstacles can also serve as a stepping stone to live a life of purpose and productivity even while healing from social hurt and racial injustice.

As God has honored me to be the author of this book dedicated to the memory of my dad, I am determined to flow in my purpose to promote, exhort, and teach racial reconciliation. My personal testimony is a testament to encourage and empower broken and hurting people despite race, creed, or color to embrace the healing power offered to us by Jesus Christ. It is my heart's desire this book will raise the reader's awareness of personal brokenness and the understanding that the path leading to wholeness is paved with repentance, self-acknowledgment, confessing your faults, the beat of a new heart, and a change in the journey of life!

Dad's Story

I HOPE THE STORIES about my dad and the spiritual transformation he and I both experienced that are contained in the pages of this book will touch your heart as well as your emotions and seal any doubt in your mind that Jesus loves and cares for you. It does not matter what the color of your skin or economic status are. He simply *cares* for you in the best of times as well as the absolute worst, downtrodden times of your life. If Jesus did it for me and my family, I know he will do the same for you and yours. God bless.

CHAPTER 1: EARLY CHILDHOOD AND GRANDPA HENRY

Plow Up the Ground

"If there is no struggle, there is no progress. Those who profess to favor freedom, and yet depreciate agitation, are men who want crops without plowing up the ground . . ." — Frederick Douglas

THE YEAR WAS 1937, a time of struggle and oppression. My father was about five years old, and he lived with his mother, six of her eight brothers, and her parents. The living conditions were deplorable. There were eleven adults plus my dad living in a four-room shotgun style house. Dad used to say you could stand at the front door and throw a rock out of the back. The plumbing and electrical work was substandard. The house became an oven in the summer and an ice capade in the winter.

Adjacent to the house was an alley where people dumped garbage and urinated, so that stench was always in the air. Dad remembered two things that he said hung as heavy as fog in a low-lying valley, and that was the smell of the alley and being hungry. Altogether, the family had ten children with seven of them still living at home. Two of the eight brothers had died a few years earlier—one from scarlet fever and the other from falling off the back of a pick-up truck. A younger daughter had committed suicide by drinking sulfuric acid. There was always a cloud of mystery that surrounded her death. Whenever anyone questioned why or how her death happened, no one wanted to talk about it. The family never talked about her life, much less her death.

Dad's biological makeup was not typical either, especially for that day and time. His mother was White, and his father was Black, but he never knew who his father was or anything about him. The fact of the matter was it was ultimately life-threatening in that day and time for a Black man to acknowledge he fathered a child with a White woman.

In the 1930s, Jim Crow laws, with all its inhumane treatment of Black people, ruled rampantly in the South. Segregation was a comfortable lifestyle for the majority of White people, and any type of interracial relationship was kept secret and considered taboo. If the secret was ever uncovered, it could mean a matter of life and death.

Dad's family was extremely poor and lived in a run-down neighborhood that was predominantly Black. It really was not unusual for poor Whites to move through and live there for a while. No matter how much better off poor Whites thought they were than Blacks, each one seemed to be dumped into an economic vice where their survival skills were put to the test daily.

Oftentimes, the suppressed neighborhoods Dad grew up in were filled with unemployed, uneducated residents who succumbed to lower-wage jobs that barely covered their needs. This economic spiral left Dad's family along with many other families wrapped in the arms of despair that regularly turned to alcohol and drugs.

As the country suffered through the Great Depression, economic conditions worsened, and the outlook became bleaker. Dad's poor, dysfunctional family unit struggled to survive and move forward while the wound of the family's personal tragedies never seemed to heal. The mystery behind how his mother's sister died has always intrigued me. Dad was so young when she died, and he told me he did not remember her.

I've wondered if her desperate last plea for help ultimately ended in her choice to kill herself—or even worse . . . in a violent act of rage, someone killed her. Could she have been more intricately connected to Dad than anyone was willing to admit? The theory that she was Dad's real mother has always been in the back of my mind. It at least justified the insensitivity and loveless manner in which the woman Dad believed to be his mother treated him. Nevertheless, it was not unusual for anyone caught up in an interracial relationship to end up missing or worst-case scenario, dead!

Even though Dad was young, he never forgot the feeling of being unloved, racially profiled, and victimized due to systemic racial inequality and the struggle to overcome economic hopelessness. I now realize the urgency with which he emphasized to me and my siblings the importance of getting a proper education. He believed education was knowledge, and that was the key to escape the bondage of the impoverished lifestyle he endured while growing up.

As a young family man during the urban renewal projects of many Black neighborhoods in the 1960s, he realized the importance of finding a niche to fit into the supply and demand economy, enhancing his skills to work in construction. He gleaned as much work skill knowledge as he could retain working on construction jobs. His goal was to one day own his own construction company. In the end, he accomplished that goal.

During the 1960s and 1970s, the demand for concrete paving became very prominent. Dad became a very sought out concrete contractor that prospered from obtaining the smaller jobs that most large companies did not have the time and patience to handle. He carved out his niche and a piece of the financial pie by gathering the crumbs of jobs that no one else wanted. He worked toward perfecting each job. So, it's not surprising it was in Dad's DNA, and he was so like his grandfather, the patriarch of his family, Henry Swopshire.

Grandpa Henry refused to give in and buckle beneath the odds. After all, his Grandfather Henry Swopshire had talked of how he had been a young soldier in World War I and had witnessed many atrocities. He guided the family to accomplish daily basic tasks despite new challenges each day.

One fond memory that Dad often spoke of was gathering food at the market with his grandfather. The farmers' market was a gathering place where farmers brought in their harvest to sell. The area bustled with activity. The smell of cucumbers and fresh fruit overlaid with sweat from anxious farmers hustling in their goods slivered through the air. Grandpa Henry would leave early enough that the crowds would have not yet arrived. He always chirped out the saying that the early bird always caught the worm.

Grandpa Henry was a stern looking man, resembling an Amish preacher, with a long beard and mustache. He always kept his mustache trimmed and waxed so that it turned up at the end in the shape of a handlebar. Going to the market was a highlighted event for Dad. He loved being and doing things with his grandfather. Grandpa Henry was very crafty with his hands and could build just about anything he envisioned in his mind. He once boasted to Dad about building the covered wagon the family traveled in from Kentucky to Texas. This creativity amazed Dad as he observed the way Grandpa Henry cut out and whittled a simple piece of wood into a handy gadget for a tool around the house or a toy for his grandson to play with for a period.

Dad acquired a lot of his creativity and craftiness from Grandpa Henry. When I look back over my childhood, I could always count on getting what I wanted in the way of toys and things. Sometimes I didn't get *everything* I wanted, but that was no big deal to me; I could always count on Dad to come through with something else in its place. He would just make me something out of scraps he gathered from various jobs he had worked on.

For example, one summer, there was the swimming pool that Dad made from scraps of plastic. My siblings and the neighborhood kids would take turns holding up one side of it to keep the water from spilling out, but it supplied us with hours of fun on a hot summer day. Even better was the Christmas that I asked Santa for a swing set and never received it, but to my surprise, I instead found a big black tire with a rope tied around it and thrown over a pine tree in our backyard. That tire was so enormously large that it had to have come from a semitruck. No swing set could have cradled me like that big rubber tire did.

On this one particular market day, Grandpa Henry made a pushcart out of old parts from a Ford Model T especially for Dad to ride in while he gathered vegetables at the market. It resembled a modern day make-shift chariot, and Dad imagined he was the Lone Ranger being pulled by his trusted horse Silver, rescuing good guys from the villains and merrily singing the theme song much to the dismay of some and the delight of others. Dad had very fond memories of the fun he experienced as his grandfather whisked him around in that little pushcart at the market. Ironically, many good memories were outnumbered by the horrific scenarios that would try to crush that little boy's hope of ever living a normal life. A life that over time beat the odds which plagued his family dynamic.

Busily, Grandpa Henry gathered tomatoes and vegetables that were overly ripe and had spots on them. No one would purchase these vegetables and, by some standards, were not even fit to eat. However, Grandpa Henry was a specialist at making vegetable soup. He would bring overripe vegetables home, separate the bad parts out of them, and place them in a big wash pot. There was never enough money to purchase meat for the soup, so Grandpa Henry would gather soup bones or cow bones to use in place of meat. He busted the bones with an ax and scraped out the marrow on the inside to season the soup. Watching this whole process filled Dad with admiration and awe. He loved watching all of Grandpa Henry's various skills including this newest one of making this tasty soup. Learning this was a valuable lesson on how to make do with what you have.

Grandpa Henry did most of the cooking while his wife Martha, and daughter Maggie (my dad's mother) cleaned and did most of the housework. Grandma Martha was the disciplinary figure in the family. She was a small woman in stature but walked tall as far as setting and enforcing rules and regulations. She was not affectionate toward Dad and the only way he escaped her wrath most of the time was to run into the loving arms of Grandpa Henry. As long as he stayed close to the loving, protective embrace he found in Grandpa Henry's arms, his world was safe and secure.

There were six boys in the family. Henry, Silas, John, Fred, Arthur, and Jim. Arthur, Silas, and Jim were the more stable ones of the brothers. Arthur was the third from the oldest and was the athlete of the family. He was big, brawny, and playful. He often pretended that he was the world's wrestling champion and Dad was his not-so-likely-to-win opponent. They worked jobs here and there, but none of them really had a regular job. No one had a formal education, and not one member of the family ever received a high school education. Education was not exactly at the top of the family's priority list.

The other three brothers, John, Fred, and Henry Jr., drank heavily and were very prone to domestic violence. Fred was the leader of the three and was very rebellious and unreliable. These three brothers very rarely contributed to the family's struggle for survival and would waste their money on beer and moonshine.

After a night of heavy drinking, Uncle Fred would stumble home bullying and verbally abusing Maggie with racial slurs of "nigger lover with a little bastard half-breed child." After a few minutes, the abuse intensified and inevitably ended in a physical altercation between Maggie and Uncle Fred. Uncle Fred really had a bitter taste in his mouth for Dad which intensified the more he drank. He stared at Dad the same as a crouched leopard lies in wait for prey. Dad was much like the helpless prey that unknowingly had no clue where the crouched leopard would lurk next, and well, let us just say Dad could sense and almost smell the terrifying fear of him.

In the back of his mind, Dad knew that one day he would have to face this fear head on. Could he survive being put to the test? Waking up from sweltering dreams that Uncle Fred would one day kill him in his sleep were just the beginning of Dad's haunting childhood memories.

CHAPTER 2: SCHOOL DAYS

Knowledge is the Key

"The individual who can do something that the world wants done will, in the end, make his way regardless of race..." — Booker T. Washington

THE NEIGHBORHOOD CHILDREN DAD played with were mostly Black. He related to and felt more comfortable around them and often dreamed about being a part of a Black family. He had several cousins that were White, but there was always tension and a sense of not belonging that tore at Dad's heart when he was around them.

He had a copper complexion, and his mother often grilled into him that if anyone approached him about his nationality, he should tell them he was Mexican. The paranoia this story produced in Dad was frustrating and overwhelming for him. It made him revert into his own imaginary world where he felt secure and less stressed about the color of his skin. I cannot imagine what it must have been like to constantly stay defensive about my appearance. One story Dad shared with me was somewhat humorous; it happened one day when he was about ten years old.

His chore was to walk about a mile to obtain water from a well. It was during this daily chore that he met his first buddy. When Dad saw this figure of a boy coming toward him, his first tormenting thoughts were that maybe this guy wants to fight. He was the same size and height as Dad. As he approached closer, Dad began to hear his mother's scripted message about being of Mexican descent. Surprisingly, the boy said, "Hi my name is Billy, you want to try a chew of tobacco?"

Dad said an abrupt, "Yes!" Suddenly the boy reached into his boot and pulled out a pocketknife out of the side of his boot. Dad was in complete amazement. He had never witnessed anything like that before, and it really caught him by surprise. The boy cut a section of the tobacco and put it in his mouth and began to chew it. By this time, Dad was beyond curious, so he asked the boy how it tasted. Billy began to laugh out loud so heartily that Dad could no longer contain his curiosity, so he grabbed a piece and began to chew it.

As he chewed the tobacco, he swallowed the juice. Billy asked if Dad wanted something to go along with it. He reached into his pocket and pulled out a round tin box. He pinched off what he called snuff and placed it inside his lip. He explained that he was doing what was called "dipping snuff." Dad was utterly amazed by all this as Billy continued to pull more and more tricks, so to speak, out of his pocket.

By now, he had taken some paper and began to roll up some of the tobacco into a cigarette. He asked Dad if he wanted a smoke. It was apparent to Dad that he was so dizzy that he could barely stand up, but unwilling to appear to be a chicken, he abruptly said, "Yes!" As he took a few puffs, he suddenly realized the amount of time he had spent with his new buddy had been too long. Reluctantly, he said goodbye to Billy and headed back home.

By the time Dad made the journey back home, he had stumbled so badly most of the water he originally was supposed to bring back had spilled out of the pail. When questioned about the water, Dad tried to cover up his newfound discoveries, but it was apparent something was different about his demeanor. His grandmother immediately began to look inside his mouth. It was like she knew just what he had done. A hearty chuckle of laughter embraced Dad as he described how she must have had eyes in the back of her head. The disciplinarian that she was, she immediately proceeded to heat up Dad's backside with a leather strap.

Grandmother Martha was a very stern and proud woman. According to Dad, she never showed a glimmer of any kind of feeling, whether good or bad, toward him. His description of her was almost as if she were numb on the inside. I could sense the sadness Dad felt in his heart when he spoke about her. He yearned for her to love him and make him feel accepted and worthy as part of the family. I think about the words found in the Bible in 1 Corinthians 13:4–7 when it states:

"Love is patient, love is kind. It does not envy, it does not boast, it is not proud. It does not dishonor others, it is not self-seeking, it is not easily angered, it keeps no record of wrongs. Love does not delight in evil but rejoices with the truth. It always protects, always trusts, always hopes, always perseveres" (NIV). These words capture the essence of what love truly is and can be, especially in the life of a young child. As I listened to Dad express the cold relationship he experienced with his grandmother, I only felt more determined to show my own future grandchildren the kind of warmth and love so necessary for them to feel safe, protected, and worthy of my unconditional love.

Summer was slowly ending, and fall was quickly making its way into the lives of family activities. School was about to open its doors for another year of learning and meeting new friends. It was not a surprise that education was not a top priority for the Swopshire family. The only subject they seemed to be highly educated in was survival skills. Nevertheless, Dad held onto the sheer hope that somehow there would be an exception for him.

I have often wondered how he kept his optimism during this time. He shared another story of feeling completely desperate for help. As I write these words it is heartbreaking for me to comprehend a young child facing an emotion as intense as being desperate for help. There had been numerous obstacles he faced in his day. He sat down on some stairs of an old building when he heard a voice whisper inside him that he was going to be all right and that he would not have to feel hopeless anymore. It would not be the last day his back was up against the wall, but he now possessed something he did not have before: assurance that something—or better yet, someone—had his back!

Chapter 3: New Friends

Making Discoveries for Yourself

"We get closer to God as we get more intimately and understandingly acquainted with the things He has created. I know of nothing more inspiring than that of making discoveries for one's self . . ." — George Washington Carver

FRIENDSHIP IS SO IMPORTANT and necessary, but in my dad's case, it was also a necessity to compensate for not having a healthy, supportive family. The Bible states in Proverbs 17:17 (NIV), "a friend loves at all times, and a brother is born for a time of adversity." Adversity was a part of life for Dad. Nothing meant more to him than the companionship of a friend.

I think of another Scripture, Proverbs 27:17 (NIV), which also states, "As iron sharpens iron, so one person sharpens another." This Scripture really speaks clearly to me that you must recognize a true friend. A true friend will simply make you desire to be a better person. A person that can smile just as bright in the good times as well as the bad. I have found that friendship on a spiritual level in my relationship with Jesus Christ.

Dad's nearest neighbors had four horses, and his grandfather used them to plow up their garden. The neighbor's son was about five years older than Dad, but that did not make any difference to him— they quickly became fast friends. The neighbors were the Birchfield family and, eventually, became the only source of family my dad would know.

As another year came and left, Grandpa Henry started to become sick. Dad developed a personal and working relationship with the Birchfields and started spending a great deal of time with them. By this time, all Dad's uncles had left home except two—one being his mean-spirited Uncle Fred. Maggie had run off with a man from Texas and left the responsibility of raising Dad to her aging parents.

Each day, Dad found himself spending more and more time at the Birchfield house. It started out to be two days at a time, then a week, until finally it became all the time. It was a season of stability for him. He ate better at their home, and for the first time in his life, he felt like he was not a problem to his grandparents, especially since Grandpa Henry's health had taken a turn for the worse.

The Valentine family was another neighboring family who lived close by. There were four children in that family—three girls and one boy. One of the girls had a defect in her eye and was teased by the other children. Her name was Wanda. She and Dad immediately developed a remarkably close relationship. At first, it was simply because she stood up for herself and fought her way through life. As Dad observed her character, he understood that just because she had a physical defect reflecting a different appearance, that did not mean she could be pushed around. She was sassy, and her presence was made known to all when she came around.

The similarity of being different in physical appearance reached out to Dad and made him realize she was a little different too, but she had a voice and a presence. Dad appreciated her boldness and strength. She was very protective of him, and overtime, he grew to love her like an older sister. She was definitely the friend that cared and stuck up for him. Even though Scripture says a brother is born for a time of adversity, Dad felt in his heart he had a loving sister.

Consequently, he was happy to finally feel a sense of belonging around others who seemed to also care about him. Just for a moment, he felt safe.

Prayer meetings were always held at Mrs. Birchfield's house. Their church was located about four miles away, and Dad attended Sunday school there. Mrs. Birchfield was a rather large woman, which probably contributed to her diabetes. She played the old pump organ for the church, but oftentimes, her legs and feet were so swollen that Dad would get under the organ and pump the pedals with his hands for her. Longing to be loved by a mother figure, he sought desperately to please Mrs. Birchfield. His heart was set on doing just about anything he could to accomplish this task. Pumping the organ for her was the first of many caregiving tasks Dad would provide for his self-obtained mother, Mrs. Birchfield— he lovingly called her Virgie.

Dad was already somewhat late starting school; however, he hoped to attend the small southern elementary school so many of his newfound friends attended. He was so excited to finally be involved in a normal child activity. He noticed Virgie and her husband, Mr. Birchfield, whisper and talk about him attending school. There seemed to be some sort of problem, but he could not see how he fit into the scenario. Virgie always assured him there was not a problem and that he should not be nervous or afraid about attending school. Dad was beyond excited!

He eagerly washed his own clothes and put the best spit shine that an eleven-year-old could muster up on his shoes. The long-awaited school day had finally arrived, and Dad was breathless to be a participant in the day's activities. He happily walked along the long road with his friends to catch the bus. Everyone told him he looked nice. He even met new friends he had not seen before. A whirlwind of dust flew from the tires of the bus as it traveled along the long and curvy backwoods road. Dad could still sense some icy stares and hear the occasional slur of the word "nigger" rise from the crowd; however, his friends Billy and his sassy, mouthy, big sister Wanda quickly squashed any perpetrator who dared cross the line.

When the bus arrived at school, Wanda hovered close to Dad, making sure that he was taken to his designated classroom. As the teacher came nearer to Wanda, she quickly gave the teacher a folded piece of white paper. Unbeknownst to Dad, Virgie had written it and asked Wanda to deliver it as soon as he was admitted to class. Wanda quickly disappeared from the classroom. Dad could tell the teacher's facial expression changed to reflect confusion, but she tried to smooth out her furrowed brow not to show it. She quickly gathered herself, smiled, and showed him to a seat in the classroom.

Throughout the day, Dad noticed people peering in the small window over the red, wooden classroom door. A sharp pain of anxiety began to nip at his stomach. He assessed the room and realized that no one else there looked like him. As the day marched on, his feelings of unease began to diminish slowly. The bell rang, and with a sigh of relief, he realized the first day of school was actually complete without an altercation. It felt good and was almost too good to be believable to Dad. Wanda had protected and saved his plight by delivering the infamous note to the teacher. Once again, it was his love for his big sister that soothed all his concerns and fears for that glorious day. It felt good. . . . It felt like acceptance. . . . Finally, he was feeling complete and whole. Upon his arrival back at the Birchfield's home, Dad was excited to tell Virgie that his day went well and his teacher was very nice to him.

The next day, the stares of the people peering in from the window above the red, wooden classroom door were more threatening and intense. No longer were they just appearing here and there. Stares of disapproval and, simply, stares of hatred were everywhere he looked. The school bell rang with a loud clang to end the day. Wanda appeared at Dad's classroom to escort him to the school bus once again.

As they approached the door leading outside, they saw three men watching each child walk past them. A deep sense of dread gripped Dad as he and Wanda slowly approached these men. He sensed these men were looking for him. His feeling was confirmed as he heard one man say, "This is the one I was telling you about, Doc!" The man grabbed Dad by the arm and spun him around. By the time he reacted, the man grabbed the side of his face and clamped on to his jaw so tightly it began to ache. Another man looked at his scalp and peered at the palms of both hands. The man named Doc began to question Wanda about what his parents looked like. She replied that his grandparents were the White German family that lived in the neighborhood.

Dad was haunted by the memory of Doc screaming out, "I don't care who they are! Don't send him down here anymore!" Adding fuel to the fire, a heated argument between Doc and the other two men began to flare about allowing him to get back on the bus. The very reality of that pierced Dad to his core.

He was so far away from any familiar landmark. He could only focus on the fact that he did not know his way back to the Birchfield's house. He could feel his heart thumping through his chest. He longed to cry as the lump in his throat expanded. He tried swallowing without it being obvious that he was at the point of crying hysterically but instead reminded himself that he should not be surprised this feeling of not belonging had once again hit him squarely in the face. This volatile incident was an ugly one-on-one encounter with hatred.

My dad later on in years expressed to me his initial thought of disbelief. How could this happen? "These people didn't even know me!" he exclaimed. "The only thing moving them to act in such a horrible fashion was that I looked different because of the color of my skin." At that moment, the only thing I could do for my dad was hug him. He needed my hug that day, but somehow, I knew it still could not be a substitute for the hug a young, scared boy needed so long ago.

He had grown to expect the name calling, stares, and sneers from his peers. But no! This event with the three men was somehow different. These three men had defiled my dad's identity as a human being and left ugly handwriting on his back labeling him unworthy. Reality began to settle into his consciousness about his identity and his status in society. Many events and things had happened in the past, but he could always move past the outcome. He had not let those things impact him too much; however, this rejection he suffered through that day was beyond any other obstacle he had ever faced. Dad's struggle to understand the whys and what ifs of this one isolated event became a life-long nightmare in his life that held him prisoner to his emotions for many years to follow.

Watching my dad go searching for answers years later about that terrible incident at school that day was not easy for me. I cannot remember a time in his life the hurtful root of that incident did not impact his thought process. There were times the anger down inside his heart bubbled up so fiercely it had nowhere to go but erupt like a volatile volcano. The struggle for his identity as a viable human being was overwhelming and destructive to his self-control on many occasions. The effect this destructive behavior had on our entire family to this day is still subject to the healing process. It is no secret to me that healing was the missing ingredient that was lacking in Dad's life during his young adulthood.

Early on, it became apparent to me that the unhealed soul walks around leaking onto anyone standing in the way. The cut of social injustice and racial discrimination continued to bleed in my dad's heart, but I could not allow that to spill over into my heart chambers. I will not lie and say it was an easy thing for me to overcome because it was not.

In 1966, I was in the sixth grade. The entire world of education came to a screeching halt. Lyndon B. Johnson was president of the United States The system of racial segregation and discrimination that comfortably fit the southern state of Tennessee was replaced by the social reform system of integration. President Johnson also signed the Civil Rights Act into law. This law outlawed discrimination based on race, color, religion, sex and national origin. There were also other distinguished men like Supreme Court Justice Thurgood Marshall who was the first Black Supreme Court Justice to serve. He was a forerunner for racial equality and had argued the way toward eliminating racial inequality in the education system. He fought for equality not only for education but housing and transportation. It was the beginning of a new era—not only for this part of the world. Consequently, my individual world would be rocked in the most uncanny way possible . . . the school I would attend was the very school that had humiliated and thrown my dad out years before!

CHaPTer 4: Race Wars

The Power of Hope

"As long as hope remains and meaning is preserved, the possibility of overcoming oppression stays alive . . ." — Cornel West, *Race Matters*

I REMEMBER A VERY distinct conversation I had with my dad about his identity. He was so conflicted as to which racial category he belonged to that he forgot about what a wonderful human creation he was. He did not feel accepted by either ethnic or racial group and this often blinded him to his own significance. As he spoke to me that day, I could sense the one thing he truly longed for was acceptance. Over the years, I have learned that we were fearfully and wonderfully created by the Creator to be unique in our own way . . . even down to our fingerprint (Psalms 139:14). We are all unique in our own way . . . the way God created us to be for a purpose!

After that horrible incident at school, Dad explained to Josh and Virgie the details of that terrifying event when he returned home. To his surprise and dismay, their reactions were not what he had expected. They did not get upset, nor did they show very much concern. Dad's entire wall of security had been shattered, and all they wanted to talk about was Mr. Lee, the truant officer!

Once again, Dad's emotions bubbled to the surface. Didn't they see the hurt on his face as he described how he had been publicly humiliated that day? Could they just once try to understand how scary it is to be singled out because of the way you look? Was anyone listening or trying to understand what happened that day?

Dad's first thought was to retreat, get by himself, and pull his emotions inward as he had often done while living with his grandparents. He asked to be excused for a little while. Suddenly Virgie angrily shouted out, "You need to do your chores first!" Crushed by her reaction, Dad tried to get a handle on his thoughts but quickly resolved his only purpose was to take care of the cows and chickens, clean the house, and carry in firewood. Downcast in his spirit, he quickly finished his chores and retreated to the woods to think about a plan on what he would do next.

He had a special place to play in the woods when he wanted to get away and be alone. It was a place his imagination could roam freely without thought to consequences or circumstance. He imagined himself as the commanding officer and the sticks were his soldiers. In his imaginary world, he had the power to wipe his enemies out at any given moment. Still, lingering thoughts of worthlessness nipped at his rational understanding.

A flood of raw emotions fueling feelings of hate constantly tried to invade his mind. He resolved to hate everybody—even the people who were good to him. Heck, he even wanted to hate Pee-Wee, the Birchfield's dog! His mind became a battlefield, the sole survival depending on him coming to some mindful understanding. Just where did he fit? What was his status in this family, in this community, even in the big, hard, cold world?

A couple of honest, soul-searching facts became apparent to him. He had to get revenge on the people who had been so mean to him. How in the world could he do this? He did not know very many Black people, and the White people he did know could not be trusted.

Just listening to Dad express his mistrust of everyone around him challenged me to understand how he survived that kind of emotional pain. I thought about my own childhood and, like most children, questioned why adults do what they do, but for Dad this was awfully hard.

I think the difference for me was I was confident my parents loved me. Dad never experienced that confidence and assurance, especially from his mother. I believe this dynamic left an everlasting impact on his life. He often retreated and found solace in his own imagination. Marcus Aurelias once said, "Pain is neither intolerable nor everlasting if you bear in mind that it has its limits and if you add nothing to it in imagination." My dad's interpretation of this very often led him to a pit of loneliness and positioned him against the world.

Two days after the school day incident, the truant officer came to the Birchfield home. He came in and they asked Dad to go outside and play. Dad could not resist his curiosity, so he crawled back into the basement window and listened. During the conversation between Mr. Lee and the Birchfield's, he could hear Mr. Lee advise them to seek out a Black family for Dad to live with. He strongly advised them to never let Dad return to the school for his own safety. Dad could hear Josh stand in his defense suggesting that he was a smart boy and would not be a problem; however, Mr. Lee admitted due to Dad's alleged ethnicity, he had no authority to make him go to a school.

Listening to the conversation between the Birchfield's and Mr. Lee thrust Dad into thinking he was inferior to everyone. He once again began to think that his only worth was to work in the Birchfield's yard building flower rock gardens and helping them to gather rocks to secure their house during inclement winter weather. Day after day, Dad's anger began to rise up over inferior feelings, and for the first time, he began to feel the emotion of hate take precedence over his thinking. All he could think about was revenge.

At the local mechanic's garage, he often accompanied Josh working on cars, and he would hear murmurs of conversation regarding a race war. He began to fear about what would happen to him in the event a war broke out. He often heard people use the word "nigger," and he began to question his identity. Even though some people acted nice toward him, his ability to trust anyone was very strained. It seemed the same people who shouted out racial slurs were also the folks that passed down their discarded clothes and shoes to him. When they were in good humor, he was labeled as a Mexican, but when they were angry with him, he became known as "that little nigger."

The fear and thoughts of a race war breaking out overwhelmed Dad sometimes. The most crippling thought was whose side he would commit to. Would they accept him as a part of the group? Watching my dad still grapple and struggle to understand and resolve this childhood trauma as an adult was heart piercing to me.

Unfortunately, it is also an issue that I too have faced amid the racial tension that still exists in the world today. My hope and consolation are found in understanding that regardless of the color of skin, we all have one common denominator: we are all human beings. Creation of mankind was intentionally thought out by our Creator. Genesis 1:27 (NIV) states, "He made mankind in his own image both male and female." Therefore, humans were all created equally and are all the same. All blood runs red! Unfortunately, our society and culture has been tainted with greed, power, lust, love of money, and a sense of superiority of one another.

Amazingly, because of my faith, as I have faced this ugly issue of racial tension, I am confident in my identity as a child of God. I believe. The words as they are stated in Scripture: "and whatever you do, whether in word or deed, do it all in the name of the Lord Jesus, giving thanks to God the Father through Him" (Colossians 3:17 NLT).

CHaPTer 5: Revenge IS Mine, SaITH THe Lord

Defined by Anger

The early blows to my psyche were not Black or White. They were Black and White . . . and I loathed them equally. — Bernestine Singley, Children of the Dream: Laurel Holliday

JANUARY 6, 2021, WAS a day my eyes were opened to an undefined reality. I watched in utter disbelief as an insurrection of our nation's capital and invasion of our democracy played out on TV before my very eyes. I could only think of the what ifs as I watched this unbelievable phenomenon play out. The more I watched what was going on, the anger in my spirit spiked an all-time high. How could this happen in 2021? It almost seemed that time regressed backward fifty years.

Yes, it is true that anger is the defining emotion of the Black experience, especially after so much injustice over so much time. I wondered how these hate-driven groups were able to even get this close to this sacred building. Just a few weeks earlier, peaceful protesters lead by Black, Brown, and White people from all over the nation peacefully came together and were attacked with tear gas and rubber bullets for speaking out against racially profiled brutality that mirrored the 1960s Civil Rights Movement.

I was a young girl at the time of this social movement, and I remember watching renowned civil rights leaders on TV such as Martin Luther King, Ralph Abernathy, Andrew Young, John Lewis, Robert Kennedy, and others as they stood against these same evil social and civil rights tactics that tarnish our society today.

Not learning from past mistakes makes it ultimately impossible not to repeat them again. At some point, mankind must evaluate what will happen if our society continues in such a barbaric way. I could not help but think of the words found in Scripture in Romans 12:19 (NIV), "Do not take revenge, my dear friends, but leave room for God's wrath, for it is written: 'It is mine to avenge; I will repay.' says the Lord." That is so crystal clear that if mankind could only let that sink in and understand that there is a price to be paid for injustice, and our Creator will be the justifier.

As stated in Deuteronomy 32:35 (NIV), "It is mine to avenge; I will repay. In due time their foot will slip; their day of disaster is near and their doom rushes upon them." These are the words that God spoke and meant for our journey of life to follow; however, mankind has set a precedent by deciding to move forward, placing seeds of discord, greed, power, the love of money, hatred, and evil doings as a basis to live. What better way to break away from this captivity than to make a determination in your mind, body, soul, and spirit to deny this way of living?

Jesus spoke to his disciples in a humbling prayer that suggested that they should forgive others before they ask for their own forgiveness from God the Father. That is hard to deal with especially when there has been so much targeted pain and suffering on disenfranchised and marginalized people for hundreds of years. It obviously will take a great deal of intentional focus on overcoming many obstacles for the transformed mind of the overcomer no matter the color of skin.

I believe there is only one way to turn around and live in a different manner, and that is to surrender your heart to Jesus Christ! The freedom this kind of confident victory brings cannot be manufactured in a pill, smoked in a marijuana cigarette, or drunk in a wine glass.

Many times, people of mixed race have identity issues. That demon plagued my dad's life, and he struggled for years. The good thing is in his struggle and his brokenness, he found hope in the end by knowing who he belonged to all alone.

Today, as I write the stories of his life, I know that same confidence that he finally found! I know that I am a daughter of a king.

As time moved forward, Dad's anger and rage about his environment continued to fume. He began to feel used only for work around the Birchfield's home, much like a house servant. He longed to be a part of a loving, nurturing family, but reality told him otherwise. He felt useless, reminding himself often that he could not even count beyond ten, nor did he know the alphabet or how to read. All he could think about was revenge, but how would he do it?

Dad was a constant companion to Josh, the Birchfield's son. He spent his spare time watching him work on cars at the neighborhood garage. Oftentimes, people would stand around and talk about "the niggers" and how there would be a war coming soon. Dad wondered what would happen to him when that time came. He began to wonder if there was anyone he could trust and ally with.

As the following winter approached, Virgie was getting sicker because of her diabetes. He was now expected to do the washing and help with the cooking along with his other chores. His day consisted of getting up around 4 a.m., doing his newly assigned chores, then accompanying Josh by riding a bicycle a few miles down the road. Josh met other workers to get on a truck that took everyone to work. Dad rode the bicycle back home and rode it back to pick Josh up later in the afternoon.

This rigorous routine wore him down emotionally as well as physically. The constant pace of the work was really starting to get to him. He felt that all his life consisted of was working and serving others that went on day after day. When he was not working, he watched over Virgie by rubbing her back to make her more comfortable. The only time he got to play was a couple of hours on

Sunday after returning home from Sunday school. Dad liked going to Sunday school. He was treated nicely while he was there.

Invariably, there was always someone telling him he would go to heaven if he became a Christian like them. All he could think about was one known fact. If there were people in heaven acting anywhere near the way people he lived around acted, heaven was not for him.

Another childhood memory Dad told me about was as Christmas approached, the church gave out Christmas gifts to all the neighborhood children. Dad remembered the anticipation and excitement every child had as they happily opened gifts. Santa called out each child's name to approach him and receive their gift. When Santa finally called his name, Santa stood there motionless before he gave him a present. Later that night, he learned the present he received was actually meant for someone who had not shown up. Dad was so hurt, he began to think he could not even trust the Christmas season and the character of Santa Claus.

CHapter 6: a Personal Relationship

There is a Difference

"God loves everyone but probably prefers 'fruit of the Spirit' over 'religious nuts'..." — Anonymous

VIRGIE SUFFERED FROM SIDE effects of diabetes for the following two years. Dad constantly stayed by her side, caring for her and getting the things she needed when she needed it. She required insulin shots, so Dad learned to give her the shot she needed. He was so nervous about being punctual with his administering the shots to her that he set an alarm clock late at night so that he would stay alert to give her the shot. Some of the neighborhood ladies stopped by occasionally to help, but Dad was still required to maintain the washing, cooking, and chopping wood for the stove along with his outdoor chores.

Early one morning as Dad went in to give Virgie her shot, he felt somberness in the room. He approached her to wake her to administer her shot but noticed she was not breathing. He listened closely to see any sign that she was still breathing. He could see she was definitely not breathing. A fiercely sharp pain ripped through his heart. The only other person he felt this close to had been

Grandpa Henry, and now both people were no longer part of his life. He felt neglected and alone.

After a few minutes of disbelief, he called for Josh to come to the room. By now Dad was overcome with sadness and emotion. Josh came to him and confirmed that she had died. Her death had occurred somewhere around four or five in the morning during his routine to give her an insulin shot.

Josh asked Dad to ride the bicycle about two miles down the road to find the only neighbor with a telephone to call the undertaker. When Dad got to the neighbor's door and knocked, the neighbor angrily opened the door with shotgun in hand. When Dad explained the events of the morning his reaction changed . . . much to Dad's relief.

After the funeral, Dad told me he did nothing but sleep for a solid week. He did not want to admit it to himself, but after the suffering he witnessed, there was a sense of relief that overcame him. He could only determine this relief was for both him and her. He desperately wanted to feel he had done what was required to take care of her. Even with struggling hardship, Virgie was the only person who had shown concern and care for him when he was not feeling well during his stay at their home.

The finality of Virgie's death left Dad thinking about his own mortality. He resolved that Grandpa Henry was old in age when he died, but Virgie was much younger. He reasoned that death not only came to the old but could come for young people too. That feeling started to sit on top of his emotions, and he felt the heaviness of it every time he pondered who would take care of him if he were to get sick.

Thoughts of illness, death, and dying began to penetrate deep into his mind. Grandpa Henry and Virgie were the only two people Dad had allowed himself to open his heart and love, but now they were no longer in the world. The fear of being alone with no one to turn to became overwhelmingly hard to cope with at times.

He often expressed to me that he really wanted to take care of Virgie because she had been the only source of motherly love shown to him. He really wanted to do anything he could to please Virgie during the time he lived with the Birchfield family. Even years later, he often spoke about winning her acceptance. He would often reminiscence over the work ethic she instilled in him. This became very apparent to me when he told me the story about how strict she was about keeping his chores done routinely. Nothing was ever supposed to interrupt the daily routine of getting his assigned work done. Even when he worked extra hard and completed his work earlier than the routine called for, he was always expected to search out something extra to do. Ironically, years later, that very same gruesome work routine would pay off for my dad's future and his legacy to his grandchildren and great-grandchildren.

CHaPTer 7: MakInG EnDs MeeT

Don't Think of Today's Failures

"Think not of the failures of today, but of the success that will come tomorrow . . ." — *Hellen Keller*

R ESOURCES WERE RUNNING LOW, and times at the Birchfield's home after Virgie's death were hard. Dad struggled emotionally to understand his place without her and her hardnosed structure and organization. This process appeared to be a thing of the past. There was only enough food for one meal and that was usually beans, cornbread, and fatback meat . . . maybe an onion sometimes.

Josh had a brother named Bill that worked on a sand barge and lived on a houseboat on the river. Dad and Josh began to hang around the houseboat at night because Bill also sold moonshine liquor. Dad really liked going to visit Bill on the boat, mainly because of the interesting people he met. He loved their clamor of conversation and fellowship with one another. He loved watching their interactions with one another. He observed them fish together and listened to the funny stories they would tell each other. For the most part, the boat environment was warm and inviting to Dad. It felt like he had stepped into a different world . . . almost as if he had been freed from the hardness of the real world.

Bill's wife was genuinely nice to him and provided a decent meal for him. She did not try to tell him when he could go and come. Instead, she made a deal with him to hunt whiskey bottles and wash them out. She gave Dad money for helping her out on this task. He started to feel a new sense of freedom that was quite different from what he was accustomed to and what Virgie had taught him.

One day, Josh informed Dad that he was staying home and did not want to go down to the boat. Dad was overwhelmingly disappointed because the boat and all his newfound friends and activities were becoming a pleasure to participate in every day. The disappointment of not going to this paradise was too much for Dad to accept. He decided to go on the cherished adventure without Josh. The trip was not going to be easy, but Dad was determined to not miss out on any of the adventurous activity.

He had to walk at least five miles or more, but he finally arrived amid the cold temperatures of the winter day. He remembered a couple of warm areas located on the boat. As he arrived, he couldn't get to one these warm spots quick enough.

He had just arrived at the boat when the police surrounded the entire boat dock and swarmed in like bees to a beehive. Dad expressed to me these police were aggressive in their behavior. They beat Bill and aggressively handled his wife. As soon as they came upon Dad, he told me he wished he had listened to Josh and stayed away. When they asked who he was, he stammered, "I'm the paperboy here to collect!" He couldn't explain why he made this statement other than his mouth opened and that was the first thing that came out.

One of the policemen angrily looked at Dad and hollered for him to get out of there. That was just what he did. He ran like the wind and never stopped until he arrived back at the Birchfield home. The next day, he explained to Josh the events that had transpired at the boat. Josh found out that Bill and his wife had been arrested, so he posted their bail to get them out of jail. A policeman explained to Josh the city evicted them and their boat from the area.

Soon after that, Bill and his wife came to live with Josh. Just like that, Dad's adventurous life and the new friendships he made while down on the river came to an abrupt halt and were over. The result of the event that occurred did not make Dad feel good at all. After all, he enjoyed the company and the activities that occurred on Bill's boat.

Everything he embraced seemed to end up in a bad way! The reality of this frightened Dad, and he didn't like how it made him feel. Epictetus once said, "What really frightens us is not external events themselves, but the way in which we think about them. It is not things that disturb us, but our interpretation of their significance."

Dad continued to live with Josh, his brother Bill, and his brother's wife until he was about thirteen years old. One day, his mother showed up out of nowhere. I believe my dad was always conflicted about his feelings for his mother. He reasoned on one hand it was pure neglect and abandonment he felt from her, but he desired motherly love so deeply he pushed his feelings down deep to not feel the pain. Consequently, his plan was to try to love her regardless of her treatment to him and survive living each day the best way he could. At least until the next disappointing blow came around. Nevertheless, his mother persuaded him to come live with her again.

Dad struggled to make that decision because his Uncle Fred often lived there whenever he was not on a drunken binge. Dad's Uncle Fred was a very mean-spirited alcoholic with destructive behavior that intensified when he drank. Dad was very uncomfortable around Uncle Fred, and he always had the worst thoughts about him. It was hard for him to understand how anyone could be so heartless toward another family member. One quote that I often thought about stated: "to not be distracted by the darkness of others to head toward the light to be good without hesitation even when other people are not that's our job!" However, there was always a gut feeling inside Dad that these raw feelings he had for Uncle Fred would one day come to a head.

As spring approached, once again Dad noticed kids in his new neighborhood were getting ready to end another school year. It was this time of year when he always felt like an oddball because he couldn't attend school. One day he met a young boy named James Clabo. James was a few years older than Dad and was going to start a summer job digging cisterns for $16 apiece. He asked Dad if he would like to work with him. To Dad, that was a dream come true as he always relied on others for cash. He eagerly accepted the challenge with great anticipation.

The workload was plentiful, and Dad was thrilled that he had his own personal cash. Even though the house they lived in had no electricity or running water, he took ownership of taking care of other things like buying food and items needed around the house. One day, a cousin came to stay at their house. Dad got him a job digging the cisterns along with him and James. The work was hard, dirty, and tiring, but Dad enjoyed it simply because the direction of his life seemed to change. This was the first time he felt he was in control of what happened to him. More importantly, the positive impact of having his own money could make a difference in his toxic living environment. Finally. It opened up a way to own his self-esteem and integrity to make lemonade from the lemons dealt to him in life.

Independence and a confidence never experienced before was forthcoming as Dad was becoming more responsible for his own well-being, even though he was still a teenager at that time. He told me he felt so free working and making his own money. Unfortunately, this new sense of independence also allowed him to venture into recreational activity that probably was not the best choice for him. For example, he and his cousin would get together at Josh's house and drink moonshine whiskey and poke berry wine while Bill's wife played the guitar.

During that summer, Dad had saved about forty dollars when his Uncle Fred began to persistently ask to borrow five dollars. When he refused and mentioned that his money was being saved to buy a motorcycle, a heated argument ensued. It had been a couple of years since his Uncle Fred had last whipped him; Dad had matured quite a bit. He was much more physically strong, primarily because of the hard manual labor he worked at every day. His physical abilities had definitely changed from that of a frail little boy, but his attitude was also zero tolerance to his uncle's abusive behavior.

Dad told me that during that time of his life, he liked to fight, and he was very eager for a fight with him that day. Dad's mother happened to come into the room at the very moment Uncle Fred's persistent taunting caused Dad to explode. He proceeded to grab his Uncle Fred by the collar and punch him in the face. Uncle Fred went stumbling backward over a cane bottom chair.

A feeling of exuberant power overcame Dad's psyche, but much too soon as he turned his back to talk to Bill's wife, who had tried to intervene to stop the fight, Uncle Fred picked up a cane bottom chair and dealt a crushing blow to Dad's head. After the initial shock of the blow to his head, he tasted blood in his mouth.

Almost immediately and without thinking, he grabbed what was left of the chair and never turned loose of it. In the back of his mind, he knew this act was out of pure survival. As the blood drizzled over his face, he soon realized how bad he was hurt. He started to visualize the contents of the room, trying to remember where Josh kept his meat knives. He held on to the one side of the chair with one hand and felt for the knives behind the door with the other hand. He desperately searched for the knives, but they were nowhere to be found. Out of the corner of his eye, he spied a meat clever lying on the edge of the table. He quickly picked it up with the opposite hand and began swinging at Uncle Fred as hard as he could. Not realizing his own strength, Dad did not know he was chopping the chair with every swing. As he felt his strength weakening, his mother ran between the two of them. Right about the same time, Dad swung and cut her hand.

Uncle Fred abruptly turned loose the side of the chair he was holding and broke into a run out the house. Dad was beside himself with high emotion as Bill's wife tried to attend to his injured head and the cut on his mother's hand. As soon as the bleeding on Dad's head had eased, his first thought was to retreat to a place of refuge, which he often found in the hilly area behind their house. This place had served as a peaceful and serene place for Dad to relax, but on this day, there was nothing peaceful about his wild and anxious thoughts . . . only thoughts of how he was going to protect him and his mother from the drunken, abusive, and intrusive character of his uncle.

By now, Dad's mother had joined him at his hilly refuge. They knew there had to be a change in their living arrangements to deal with Uncle Fred's bad behavior. The more Dad thought and talked about it, the madder he became. He decided if anyone left, it would be Uncle Fred.

About that time, Dad's cousin Sam came out to talk to him about what had happened. Sam assured Dad that he would talk to Uncle Fred and sought out to start the mediation process. Sam had not been in the house five minutes when he came running out followed by Uncle Fred with a rifle snapping at Sam's back. Lucky for him, the rifle didn't have any shells in it. Uncle Fred saw the gun didn't have any shells in it, so he threw it down on the ground and went back inside.

Dad waited until it was dark to retrieve the rifle Uncle Fred had thrown down on the ground. He resolved the only way he and his mother would be safe for the remainder of the night was to arm himself with shells for the rifle. He set out to buy rifle shells from a neighborhood man Josh had always brought shells from. As he came upon the neighbor's house, he noticed the man was in his barn milking a cow. As Dad approached him, the man turned hurriedly and asked nervously what he wanted. Dad's reply was he needed rifle shells to go possum hunting. The man glanced up and jokingly asked, "You're not going to shoot anybody, are you?" Dad tried hard not to let him see his anxious emotions glaring through his eyes. The man was reluctant but eventually sold Dad the shells.

That night Dad could not run back to the hill behind his house fast enough. Unlike all the other times in the past, he was determined to not be the one to leave their house tonight. Anger and rage began to bubble up inside him as he recalled all the times his uncle had eaten all the food he brought, spent money he had borrowed from him without paying it back. And on this night, the very act of not allowing him and his mother to come back to their home . . . was unthinkable. His emotions overwhelmed him as he began to shake and feel weak.

He sensed a killing was about to happen, and if he were caught, he would surely face a horrible life of doom. Something in Dad's gut told him to not go back to the house. He made a knee-jerk decision to go to Josh's house instead. As he started to cross the field, Uncle Fred spotted him and began to run toward him yelling, "Wait a minute, you little Black son of a bitch."

Dad told me he could see something flashing in Uncle Fred's hands and it looked like a butcher knife. As Uncle Fred lunged faster toward him, he held the knife down at his side with one hand and beat his chest with his other hand. He began taunting and yelling more racial slurs and challenged Dad to shoot him. A neighborhood lady came from out of nowhere and got close enough to Dad to ask what was going on. He told her he only wanted his uncle to leave his mother's house. Dad was shaking uncontrollably by now, and the little bit of strength he had mustered up was slowly seeping out of his arms and legs.

As he told me this story, I noticed the intense emotions he must have felt that night try to return to his memory. That night was one of the turning points of Dad's life. I believe there was a covering that protected him from a brutal killing. Dad remembers the lady gently persuading him to not shoot his uncle. He told her that his uncle had a knife and that he needed to defend himself from being killed. The lady screamed at Uncle Fred to put the knife down and at Dad not to shoot him. Uncle Fred forged forward in a drunken rage, and Dad fired the first shot landing near him. The rifle was a single shot, so Dad hurriedly reloaded the gun with Uncle Fred getting dangerously closer by the minute.

Dad recounted what it would be like to kill someone. At that moment, his teeth began to chatter, and he started to sweat profusely. His legs were weak and trembling, but he knew he was a good shot. As he aimed and found his uncle in his rifle's sight, he remembered Josh telling him if he ever were in a position to shoot to kill, aim for the head. Visions of that nauseated Dad. His mind was racing, but then he remembered other advice was to shoot toward the shoulder to slow them down rather than kill them. His sight was aimed at his uncle's head, but he decided to shoot him squarely where Uncle Fred had taunted him to shoot him—in the chest!

BANG! The bullet zoomed out of the rifle's barrel and hit Uncle Fred. Dad remembered it as an out-of-body experience and, the line between imaginary and reality blurred. Dad began to run as fast as he could to the top of the hill and threw the rifle into a grove of honeysuckle bushes.

The next memory he recalled was at Josh's house confessing to killing Uncle Fred. Josh very flippantly asked him, "Well, did you make sure that you killed the son of a bitch?" As Dad reminisced on the events of that day, he remembered that it wasn't long before the police arrived at the Birchfield house. They showed up in full force carrying an arsenal of shotguns and tommy guns and were accompanied by dogs. He could see them getting out of cars and was overwhelmingly scared of what was going to happen to him next.

He explained to me that he really wanted to run but realized they probably would have no problem catching him. Surprisingly enough, they came in the house and walked right pass him and asked Josh, "Where's the nigger that shot the White man?"

Josh replied, "Leon shot him." The policeman whirled around and looked right at Dad. At that moment, Dad saw his entire short life flash before him.

With a cocky, sarcastic tone, the policeman replied, "He is just a kid!"

In a flash, another policeman grabbed Dad by the arm and said in an aggressive voice, "Where is the gun, boy?" Josh pulled the officer to the side and explained that Dad would go get the gun and bring it back to them.

A thousand thoughts crossed Dad's mind as he walked back to the honeysuckle bush where the gun he shot Uncle Fred with laid. In the distance, he could hear the freight train that ran like clockwork every day a few blocks away. The thought ran strongly through his mind to run and catch it! Suddenly a still, small, but even more convincing voice said, *No!*

Dad was taken to jail, accompanied by three policemen, as soon as the gun was turned in. Two policemen sat in the back seat of the patrol car. The policeman on his left side had a nasty attitude while the other policeman on the right side was nicer. They asked him a lot of questions, writing his answers down each time. When he arrived at jail the policemen escorted him to an office where he was left for several hours.

Finally, they put him in a cell with two old men. It seemed that every thirty minutes, someone different would come and ask him the same questions over and over. Dad explained to me that he was so exhausted that he lay down on one of the bunks in the jail cell. There were four bunks with no covers, just an iron frame with a toilet at the end. He told me that as he lay down, he noticed his head was bleeding from the violent encounter with Uncle Fred. One of the old men had a tattered handkerchief that he placed on the gash. Dad soon drifted off to sleep.

As he looked back on that day in jail, he could not remember if it was later that night or early the next morning, but he heard Josh calling his name. As he awakened, he opened his eyes to see Josh and another man standing in front of him. They had come to get him out of jail. Josh had later explained he had put the house up as collateral. Josh told Dad he was not to go anywhere because neighbors were talking about Dad shooting his Uncle Fred. He was genuinely concerned for Dad's safety and felt it better that he did not leave the house until the intensity of this incident blew over.

Dad was scared and confused about what was going to happen next. Everyone told him if his uncle died, he would assuredly go to the electric chair. He remembered his grandmother at the height of her anger often reminded him that even though he was her grandson, she believed he was a bad seed and was going to die in the electric chair before he turned twenty-one. Dad told me he didn't know what death would be like. He remembered thinking that he was so downtrodden, emotionally exhausted, and discouraged that if this happened, he wished it to happen as soon as possible because then he would not have to worry about his safety or anyone else's anymore.

Uncle Fred miraculously survived this horrible event and was released from the hospital two weeks later. He did not press charges to prosecute Dad, but he had a court hearing soon and had to be ready to speak to the judge.

On the day of the hearing, Dad was uncertain what the judge was going to do or say to him. He said he was so nervous and shaky he could barely stand up. Dad decided he would keep his eyes looking straight at the judge in hopes that he would not see how much he was shaking. The judge stared back with a look of evil superiority. Dad reasoned that the judge did not respect him as a human being, so he became determined to overcome this intimidation, which, as he explained to me, seemed to give him unexplainable strength.

Josh looked melted down with his hat in his hands and his face lowered. The judge talked to Josh as if Dad were not even standing there, and everything resolved to being a favor to Josh. The judge turned his stare back to Dad, and he asked him if he would shoot his uncle again if he had the opportunity. Out of the corner of Dad's eye, he could see Josh shake his head from side to side to motion Dad to say no. In an instance of defiant rebellion, Dad said, "Yes, I would!"

The judge raised up out of his chair and looked at Dad and sternly said, "What did you say?" Josh gave Dad a look of helplessness. Dad asked the judge if he could say something to which he swiftly said no. Josh began to plead with the judge that Dad did not mean it. The judge reluctantly turned to Dad and said, "What do you have to say?"

Dad courageously spoke up and told the judge he had to shoot his uncle because he was too weak to run. He pointed out that if he had not shot him, he would have been stabbed to death with the knife. After a short time of deliberation, the judge returned to stare at Dad and tell him that he was releasing him into Josh's custody and that he had better not ever appear back in his court or he would put him away for good. Dad resolved to never come back to court.

I believe, all anyone must do is stand up and believe that fear will not take over. My pastor teaches in many sermons that fear is a spiritual gift from the devil; send the package back!

Growing up, Dad tried to teach me how to swim, but I never learned, and I developed an intense fear of being around water. Watching other people have so much fun and enjoy being in the water has always intrigued me, but I still have this crippling fear of water. I decided to act upon this fear one day, so I bought a float to float on and enjoy the serenity and peacefulness of being in the water. As soon as I got on the float, I immediately began to think that maybe this was not a great idea. I could feel the fear creeping to the forefront of my mind, and I immediately anchored myself to the edge of the pool and docked myself to the handrail. Embarrassed and humiliated, I tried to act normal, but anyone could see my actions were not normal.

I allowed my fear to overtake me. The fear was taking my breath away when God's spirit gently whispered to me these words: "Just stand up." The fear had consumed me so quickly I had not taken the time to observe my surroundings. If I had just faced the reality of the situation, I would have realized that I was in four feet of water, and the practical thing to do was to stand up.

That day in court when my dad stood up for what he believed as he spoke to the judge, it made me realize the common denominator in these two instances is that fear must be faced and dealt with. To stand upon your beliefs even when you are afraid takes courage and strength that must be pulled from a trusted source.

The Bible states in 2 Timothy 1:7 that we are not supposed to entertain our thoughts to have fear in the first place. God did not give this feeling to us. What he did give us is the ability to control the thoughts that come to mind and our behavior as we process those thoughts.

Dad told me he could sometimes feel alone and scared in a room crowded with familiar faces but never really trusting anyone. My heart ached with thinking that he faced so many obstacles daily just to survive in his environment. He did not understand the battle he was fighting was already being won by a loving and caring God. Trust issues were always a part of his life, but as years passed he began to understand that to trust is to surrender control to someone else and believe in their reliability. He found just that someone...in *JESUS!*

CHaPTer 8: MOVING Forward

"You see things; you say, 'Why?' But I dream things that never were; and I say, 'Why not?'" — *George Bernard Shaw*

IN THE WEEKS THAT followed, Josh forbid Dad from leaving the house. The stern and grim advice the judge gave him rang in his ear day after day, but eventually, as time would have it, the reality to move forward began to sink in. He started to venture out and work for different people. He worked as a laborer doing various jobs around the community such as mowing lawns and cleaning out basements.

Dad was a maturing teenager by now, and many people questioned Josh about why he was still living at his house. It seemed that Josh was regularly confronted about their living arrangement. It became more obvious to Dad that he should start a life on his own. After all, Josh sacrificed a lot for Dad's well-being. He did not want to be the cause of any more trouble for Josh.

Early one summer morning, he set out to conquer the world on his own. As he was walking down the road not knowing where he was going or what he was going to do, a distinct voice in the distance yelled out to him. "Hey, young man!"

As Dad turned around to look, he noticed an older man motioning for him to walk closer. As he approached the elderly man, he guessed this man was a landowner by the way he was dressed and how he carried himself. He was very neat in appearance. His overalls were nicely starched and ironed. His hair was completely grayed, and his forehead was tanned around his furrowed brow line. He asked Dad if he would like to work for him cleaning out cow stalls. He also asked him if he had any knowledge about horses. Dad was confident in his knowledge about horses. It didn't take but a quick minute for Dad to accept the job offer.

The elderly man quickly assigned Dad to hook up a mule to the sled to haul manure out of his barn. He assured Dad he would have a work partner to assist him before the end of the day. Neither the fact that the job was messy and smelly mattered to Dad, nor whether or not a help mate would show up. What mattered to him was he had a legitimate job making money to help him survive on his own.

After a couple of hours, the elderly man returned with a teenage White boy about Dad's age that he also employed as a laborer. The elderly man had explained to Dad earlier that he was going to be held accountable for the completion of the job. The White boy was about the same age as Dad but a little larger, and he felt he should be in charge. Throughout the day, Dad started to reminisce on all the times Josh had told him if anyone placed him in charge of anything to always take responsibility for it.

After a short time, the White boy began to boss Dad around, shouting out where to throw the manure and demanding to drive the mule. Dad reasoned the job was his responsibility, and he was going to protect his ownership at all costs. Rage and anger overwhelmed him as they both reached the boiling point, so they started to fight. The elderly man saw them fighting and ran down to see what was going on.

After hearing both their stories, surprisingly, the elderly man sided with Dad. The White boy was somewhat resistant to this decision, but the elderly man informed him if he didn't like it, he could take a hike and leave. Dad expressed to me how his heart leaped for joy. Beginning that day, he pledged to be loyal to the elderly man that had stood up for him.

As the sun set and the day ended, Dad felt, all in all, his day had been more productive than most. He still needed to find a place to sleep and resolved in his mind that this time his place of residence would be on his own terms. He took his day's wages and purchased a tent and pitched it out in the woods.

Kids in the neighborhood started to come around if nothing else but for curiosity about Dad's latest living arrangement. To other kids, it was a playhouse, but to Dad, it was his dwelling place. It was his home. Most days after working all day, he came home to his tent, and all is food was gone and the tent would be in shambles. Much to his dismay, his new living arrangements began to be a burden to him. He knew he couldn't continue to live in the tent, but he had no idea where else he could go.

The elderly man Dad worked for observed his growing anxiety and asked him if anything was bothering him. Dad explained that the neighborhood kids vandalized his tent and ate his food each day while he was at work. To Dad's surprise, the man offered him room and board in his home with the condition he would continue to work for him.

Unfortunately, Dad did not get to move into his new room and board right away. A couple of days earlier, he noticed a bright rash had appeared on his arms and back and was growing rapidly. He decided to tell his new boss about his dilemma. The man told him he could not provide a room to him while the rash was still active. He wanted Dad to get checked out by a doctor.

The local clinic that was available catered only to the White residents in the community, but Dad decided he would take a chance and ask for treatment anyway. The next day he sat in the waiting room for several hours until the clinic was closing when the nurse finally came to the lobby and informed him the following Tuesday was nigger's day, and he should come back then.

Dad knew he had to tell his boss that he was unable to get an examination and blood test by the doctor. Not only that but it was going to take another week before he could be seen. Dad told me he was worried his boss would ask him to leave but instead he gave him a note and told him to go to his doctor's office a short distance away. The following day he went to the doctor's office. As he entered the lobby, he expected to meet the same racist resistance he had always experienced, but instead the receptionist was a nice person. The doctor read the note Dad's boss had sent him with. His attitude changed, and he seemed to act nicer after reading the note.

He soon began asking Dad a series of questions about his work conditions. Apparently, the brushy area a few yards away from his boss's barn was covered with a poison ivy vine. The nurse came in, took blood, and gave Dad a small tube of ointment for the rash. The doctor informed him he did not have a contagious disease and that he was a victim of an infected case of poison ivy. The nurse advised him the doctor would speak with his boss about his condition and advised him to use the ointment daily. As soon as he returned back to the barn, his boss told Dad he could have a room and board at his home. What a sweet relief Dad felt. At least now he would have his own room.

That year he lived with his boss and worked for his room and board. It turned out to be an eye-opening experience. Dad had been used to hard work but never to this extreme level. He started to feel discouraged and stressed out about keeping up with all his responsibilities. After the racist treatment he received from trying to get proper medical attention, he resolved that he would never go through that humiliation again. That experience made him feel less than human, and for many years after that, he never had a tolerance for doctors or medical institutions. I never saw him go to a doctor until he was well into old age.

CHaPTer 9: WInGS OF Iron

Living day-to-day

"Dig the well before you are thirsty." — *Chinese Proverb*

Wings of Iron glistening, shining in the noon day sun
How I marvel at all the things they've done
Brawny and rugged, strong and firm I can't believe
The strength they earn. Soaring thru the ages
As his will provides. Humbly and graciously
How they glide. Bow to him for birth. Bow to him for life.
Bow to the Creator that saves us from strife.
--- Yvonne Webb © 1995

D AD REMEMBERED HIS DAYS working for the elderly man and the skills he learned. He described this time as a period of transition from boyhood to manhood. The level of responsibility and accountability was higher than any other job he had worked. He told me that his day started before 7 a.m. every morning. He was accountable for making sure a large number of hogs and chickens were fed before breakfast. After he ate breakfast, he would feed and tend to several mules getting them harnessed and ready to plow the field. He explained that he never learned exactly how to properly plow with the drag harrow and disk. There was a neighborhood boy who lived nearby who could properly use the plow. He became a good friend to Dad. Together they spent endless hours plowing up the tough terrain of land. The work was backbreaking and hard but necessary for Dad to make his way in a world where the odds were stacked against him. After a hard day's work of plowing and making sure all the work animals were well maintained, Dad had very little time to do anything but fall asleep from mere exhaustion.

He would often go over events of his life and think about how he narrowly escaped dangerous situations that could have not ended well for him. He could not reason why his mother's constant abandonment of him for long periods of time was necessary. He often thought it would be better for him if he could be part of his father's world. Unfortunately, his mother did not share a lot about his father with him. Feelings of unworthiness plagued his thought processes.

One recurring thought that he always held close to his heart was the contribution he was going to make to the world. Consequently, he did make a lasting impact on everyone he met. Especially when he was able to showcase his work skills. He could not read words, but somehow, he learned to count, and he taught himself the metric system. Reading a measurement ruler came very easy for him, and he could estimate precise measurements at a glance.

As the days, weeks, and months moved along, another thought that Dad kept in the back of his mind was being adventurous. He had loved the days of living on the houseboat and being surrounded by the interesting people he met during that time. The constant force in his life seemed to be the hard work that he endured each day. He was thankful for finally having a nice living environment, but he knew somehow, he had to find a way to move beyond the constant grind of manual labor.

One day, the neighborhood boy he had befriended told him about a circus sideshow that was coming through the community. Dad had never been to anything like this, but his curiosity was piqued. He and his friend decided they would both sneak away and attend one of the sideshows. Dad's friend had heard there were ladies in the show that would take all their clothes off as soon as the music started. He and his friend could not contain their curiosity.

The following Saturday night, the sideshow and its entire entourage marched into the rural community. As soon as the sideshow booths were set up and it was dark enough, Dad and his friend hid in a desolate area at the back of one of the unoccupied booths and devised a plan to sneak into the shows. They both hid behind some barrels right outside an opening that permitted them to have a bird's eye view. The opening was just wide enough for them to get a look at activities on the inside.

Dad was awestruck at all the activities and hustle and bustle going on in the area. There were all kinds of advertisements about human oddities and daredevil stunts. Dad was particularly captivated by the speaker that stood outside the booth and challenged people walking by to come inside to see these unusual oddities for themselves. There was something about the way the speaker searched out people in the crowd and used the power of the unknown as a mechanism to lure people.

By this time, Dad's friend wanted to continue his search for the ladies, but Dad suggested they split up in their search to look for this act. Dad was completely captivated by the alluring power this speaker had over the crowd. He was completely mesmerized by the speaker's tactic of telling the crowd what they were about to see was not deemed for women and children but only for the strong. The speaker seemed to have magical powers over spiking the crowd's fear and curiosity to take a look at what was inside the show.

When Dad got back to his room that night, he could barely get to sleep. He thought about all the sights and sounds he had witnessed that night. Something inside him longed to be a part of that type of excitement. He had not felt that kind of excitement since his days on Bill's houseboat. He was smitten with all the sounds and sights, the challenge and adventure being promoted, but most of all, he was intrigued by the *power* the speaker had controlling the crowd. He knew this was a unique gift and he wanted it for himself. The next day, all Dad could think about was going back to the sideshow to listen to the speaker.

As soon as the workday ended, Dad resolved to sneak back into the sideshow where the speaker would call out to people passing by and lure them to come inside the show to witness the attraction. He later found out the proper name for the speaker was called a barker. This was a person that was very vital to the success of the show's popularity. The art of barking was a skill that needed a certain charisma. The barker would shout out, "Step right up, ladies and gentlemen, boys and girls."

On this night, Dad was particularly intrigued by this barker because he looked different, and it appeared that he was younger than the gentleman he saw the previous night. Of all things, the specific act was centered around something Dad could only imagine in his wildest dreams—a fire-eater!

Dad told me, that night he made his mind up to follow a different path for his life. He felt the only thing he was doing in life was working for other people to enjoy the fruit of his labor. He wanted to build a career centered around what he wanted to do instead of what someone else wanted him to do. He really started to feel the frustration of not wanting to do the hard manual labor necessary to keep up his chores around the elderly man's farm anymore.

A man who lived close by approached Dad one day and made him an interesting proposition. He proposed Dad a job working on his farm taking care of his hogs. He indicated he couldn't pay Dad more money, but he could have room and board free. He had two mules and would help the man plow on the side and split the money they earned from the job. It didn't take Dad long to decide he would give this new job a try because the elderly man started to take financial assessments out of Dad's pay. By the end of the week, Dad owed him too much money.

Once he reconciled his living expense charges with the elderly man, he sought out to start his new job at the neighboring farm. He struggled with disgruntled feelings with the elderly man because even though he could not read the ticket of expense charges given to him, he was really good at math . . . and the expenses didn't add up and were unrealistic. Nevertheless, Dad knew it was a battle he could not win. He paid the elderly man, gathered his few belongings, and moved onward.

He began to work for Mr. Roy, taking care of his hogs and plowing gardens. Dad was not trusting of Mr. Roy because of his latest experience working out living expense charges with the elderly man. However, Mr. Roy was faithful to split the money he made with Dad for plowing. Working with Mr. Roy became somewhat more enjoyable as they traveled around to various restaurants gathering fermented food used for slop to feed the hogs. He met people who worked in the kitchens and learned how to story tell and joke around, which always produced a good laugh.

One memory he told me about was the time Mr. Roy showed him how to set up a liquor still. Oftentimes, folks thought Mr. Roy was using the slop he gathered at restaurants to feed his hogs when really the majority of it he used to make liquor. On this one occasion, Mr. Roy decided to let Dad "run the mash," which is a process to strip the water, yeast, and sediment out of the mash before the liquor runs. Mr. Roy reminded Dad to "keep the dough around the fittings," making sure the liquor still didn't lose steam. Dad was very careful to follow the procedures Mr. Roy had instructed.

They had also killed a couple of hogs that day which were roasting in the background, and Dad had not eaten that entire day. He noticed a piece of tenderloin available to eat, so he grabbed it and began to eat it. As he sat there eating that piece of tenderloin, his mind wandered to what would happen if they were caught making liquor. With his urge to drink something to wash the tenderloin down, he decided to drink a teacup of the newly run liquor.

He drank some of the clear liquid, and it burned all the way down to his stomach. The more he drank the less it burned and the better he felt. Dad told me he remembered having a feeling of being mad and happy all at the same time. He remembers he boxed with trees in the area and kicked buckets over thinking he was playing football. He started to perspire profusely which was the last memory he had of that night.

Early the next morning, he woke up to someone saying, "Where is he at?" He had crawled up into the hog pen and gone to sleep. Mr. Roy pulled him out and made him sleep in the basement because of the stench. He was so angry about the outcome of Dad's handling of the liquor still. All the liquor had run down the hill, the fire had gone out, and the entire area was one big mess! On top of everything else, Dad was sick.

The next day, the smell was still there. The smell of spending the night with hogs appeared to not want to go away anytime soon. He took several baths, and still the odor lingered. After all these unfortunate events, Dad knew he needed to escape to a new life, totally different. The sideshow would be leaving the following weekend. He resolved a plan to leave town with the circus sideshow.

Dad decided the only chance he had was to talk to the young man he saw at the sideshow beckoning bystanders to come inside and witness the show's attraction. As soon as the show was about to end, Dad very cleverly made his way through the opening he had used to view the shows on the previous nights to come face to face with the young man. At first, he was a little nervous and intimidated by the young man he came to know later as Joe. He knew he had to take a chance and just come out and ask Joe if he could get a job with the sideshow.

He finally mustered up the words to ask him. Joe immediately asked how old Dad was. Without thinking, Dad immediately lied about his age. At the time, he was sixteen about to turn seventeen, but he said he was twenty. Joe asked a few questions about Dad's background to which Dad explained that he had no family and had basically been on his own. Joe was easy to talk to, and Dad felt comfortable around him as they talked. It is not known whether or not Joe actually believed all the personal information that Dad told him that night, but nevertheless, just like that . . . Dad was hired as a grounds keeper and to run errands. This started a new chapter of adventure in his life's journey.

The excitement grew on a daily basis for Dad as the show traveled from city to city. He and Joe became great friends, resulting in Joe teaching Dad the art of becoming a barker for the sideshows.

I remember growing up, Dad often performed some of the barking skills for me and my siblings that he acquired during his time with the circus sideshows. I was always amazed at how convincing he became as he described the mysterious attraction behind the curtain.

Eventually, Dad learned all he could learn about the entertainment industry of a circus sideshow during that time. He worked with and became friends with people who were a part of the show that exhibited human oddities such as the largest human man who weighed seven hundred pounds, the bearded woman, the smallest human—a lady who was only about three feet tall—and to top them all . . . the man who could eat fire!

I asked Dad one day about what his life was like being a fire-eater on the sideshow. He explained to me those days were filled with anticipation, excitement, nerves, and adrenaline-pumping challenges, and if he had to do it all over again, he would not change anything. He was young, single, and good-looking with his life moving in a direction that seemed promising. At least that was what he thought until it all came crashing down the night the fire-eating act went horribly wrong.

Dad explained the trick to the act was all in how he exhaled his breath to put out the flame. He never really ate the flame. He literally put the flame out by a quick exhaling breath which extinguished the flame. However, this one particular night, Dad felt his timing was off balance, and he did not exhale the flame quickly enough, causing some of the flame to fly back onto his lower neck and chest area.

Thanks to the quick action of Dad's friend, Joe, who immediately saw what was happening and extinguished the flame, it stayed away from his face. Unfortunately, the flames left second and third degree burns on his lower neck and chest area. Just like that, Dad's circus career came to a screeching halt.

Chapter 10: Till Death Do Us Part

"A successful man is one who can lay a firm foundation with bricks others have thrown at him." — *David Brinkley*

A FTER THE FIRE-EATING ACCIDENT and Dad's wounds healed, he decided to travel back to the southern part of the country. It just so happened that he came back to the same area he abruptly departed from a few years earlier. He had wanted to experience a more adventurous life before, but after the traumatic experience, he thought about his life differently. He began to think about what was most important to him and the lifestyle he wanted to live. He never once lost the longing in his heart to be surrounded by a loving family. He immediately resolved in his mind that if he had not been born into that perfect scenario, he would create that family dynamic himself.

Upon his return to the town he had practically escaped from a few years earlier, he quickly realized some things changed, but there are some things that still remain the same. He was curious about what had happened to a handful of friends and acquaintances he left behind. The pace and movement of life in the sleepy little southern town still crept along with not much of a change of mindset. This was vastly different from what he had experienced from his travel to northern cities. Nevertheless, he decided to stick around if for nothing else but to find a few friends to kick around with during his expected brief stay.

After a few days of wandering around, Dad thought it wouldn't be a bad idea to stay for a more extended time than he originally planned. I never really got the full understanding of how he wound up working at the city hospital. He told me that was really the first job that he felt like he was an official employee. He joked about having his own uniform and reporting to a person inside a building in the city. He started work there as a custodian cleaning floors on the labor and delivery section of the hospital.

His female supervisor was somewhat of a disciplinarian with lots of characteristics that mirrored Virgie's personality. She was a White woman with carrot red hair and porcelain-like skin. Her white uniform was meticulously laundered and starched. She had a strict policy that no one reporting to her unit had a dischuffed appearance. Even though she was short in stature, she ran the team of people who reported to her much like a very tall general.

She took a special interest in keeping him moving on the straight and narrow path. Dad and I always laughed hilariously at many of the experiences he had while working there. We found one particular story was not only comical but impactful enough to change the way Dad viewed himself for the rest of his life.

Dad had overslept and almost missed getting to work on time, so he decided to not pay as much attention to his wrinkled uniform as he normally would for the sake of time. When he arrived at work looking unkept and disheveled, his supervisor jumped on him like a flea to a dog. She grabbed him by the ear much in the fashion of his grandmother in one of her disciplinarian tantrums. He remembered sliding down the waxed corridors that he spent many hours waxing with this short, little White woman attached to his ear. Dad was so shocked that she had taken this approach with him that he had no choice but to surrender.

That day Dad received a tongue lashing about how he was going to be perceived through life. He could take the advice and apply it or leave it along with the unkept uniform for someone else to wear as he would be quickly relieved of his duty. Needless to say, Dad never forgot about the importance of intentionally putting priority on looking your best, especially while representing your work.

The experience working at the hospital on the labor and delivery floor also significantly impacted Dad. Each day, he witnessed new life being born into the world. He told me about the times he would go down to the newborn nursery and glance over at the newborn babies while wondering in the back of his mind if he would ever have a family of his own. He often would see the nervous new fathers staring into the window, and he could only imagine what it must feel like to be a father.

Up until this time, Dad had been leading the life of a care-free bachelor. During his travels, he met a few girls and even older women who would have jumped at the chance to become his significant other; however, he never really felt an attraction to anyone except for one young lady he met while traveling with the sideshow. She was the first girl he actually had a physical attraction to. She was a White girl with radiant piercing blue eyes and jet-black hair that hung to her waist. She was tall in stature, which somewhat bothered Dad because she was a few inches taller than him.

Dad was slightly shorter than most men, which was overly emphasized due to his muscular build. He was a very handsome man with silky dark black hair, a copper skin tone, and unique facial features reflecting his mixed ancestry. Oftentimes, people of mixed races gravitated to the race group they most looked like. Dad could have easily passed as Hispanic because of his dark straight hair, dark eyes, and skin tone. His only fault was he could not speak Spanish. But he did learn a few Spanish words and phrases, which he loved to occasionally throw around to see if he could fool anyone about his heritage.

Dad told me that his fling with his first serious girlfriend was short lived because her family strongly disapproved of their relationship. It ended abruptly when her two brothers paid a visit to Dad to give him an ultimatum: if he valued his life, he would leave town and forget about their sister, or they would make sure he would suffer. Reluctantly, he resolved to not take the brothers' demands lightly and set out to get as far away as he could. It has been said you always remember your first love. He always remembered that brief relationship with fondness.

On his off day from working at the hospital, he was sitting on the front porch of the boarding house where he lived in a rented room. He noticed a young girl skipping down the street in a backward motion. As she skipped closer to where he was sitting, he could see she was a very cute teenage girl about sixteen years old. He told me she was so cute he could not let her pass by without saying something to her. Unfortunately, when he finally said hello, she lost her balance and skipped right into a tree. Shocked by the accident he had just caused, he instinctively ran over to assist her off the ground.

She was not happy and somewhat embarrassed about what had just happened. When Dad realized she was not seriously hurt, he must have had a smirk on his face because she responded, "What is so funny?"

Quickly taking over the conversation, which seemed to be failing, Dad said, "So sorry, are you okay?"

Just like that, my mom skipped into Dad's life, and they became part of each other's lives for the next sixty-five years. As I think about the haphazard way my parents entered into each other's lives, I often wonder *what if?* If Dad would have hesitated for one moment and let that opportunity to meet Mom at that time pass, everything may have been different. One of my favorite Scriptures is Jeremiah 29:11 (NLT), "For I know the plans . . . for good and not for disaster, to give you a future and a hope." Nothing could be truer about their relationship over the years.

Dad didn't know at the time, but Mom only lived a few blocks away in the same neighborhood. His landlady was a friend to my mother's family. My parents would occasionally see each other in the neighborhood and eventually became friends. About six months later, Dad decided he would take my mother to a movie on his off day. Mom had warned him that her mother was very strict, and the only way that she would be permitted to go is he had to ask her mother for permission. Mom decided a great way for a first-time introduction would be for Dad to come to Sunday dinner.

The following Sunday as Dad got dressed for Sunday dinner at Mom's house, he started to get nervous and uncertain that he would not be accepted. Struggling with the thought of not being accepted by someone else was a dynamic that Dad had faced so many times before. By this time, he was so accustomed to it, he felt numb on the inside, and deep down, he expected the rejection.

Mom really liked him and gave him lots of hints on what to say and do around her mother. One thing she told him was to be very careful not to offend her. Mom had also warned him that her mother owned a gun that she kept under her bed mattress. That thought really started to make Dad uneasy, and for a moment he thought about just ditching the entire meet-up. The only reason he decided to follow through was Mom had really made an impression on him with her warm and witty personality. He enjoyed her company and the fun they had together. Not to mention the fact that he was so attracted to the way she looked, especially the way she wore her hair down over one eye.

Standing in front of the door of my mother's house and the journey that followed after the door opened marked a new beginning for my mom and dad. My mom was an only child, and her mother was a widow. Sadly, my mother's mother and her husband had been in a grinding car accident years before. My mother's father had been killed, and her mother was seriously injured with a leg injury that hindered her mobility for her entire life. As Dad walked into the tiny apartment, he smelled a delicious aroma that almost made him jump for joy. He had not smelled such an aroma of spices before. He later found out the dish was chicken and dumplings accompanied by sweet potato casserole, collard greens, and buttermilk cornbread. Dad told me he ate so much that day he was embarrassed to move away from the table because his pants felt extra tight and the top button was hanging by a thread.

After dinner and a brief conversation, the time came to ask about Dad taking Mom to the movies. Suddenly, my grandmother's entire countenance changed to a stern authoritative stare. She explained that Mom had a 9:00 p.m. curfew, and she was not permitted to be one minute late. If she were late, he would be accountable. Dad cautiously agreed to have her back home while all the time thinking about the gun Mom said she kept under her mattress.

Going to the movies was always a treat for both my parents. During that time, they were only permitted by law to sit in the balcony at the theater. Systemic racism separated White people from Black people. On that Sunday so many years ago, it didn't matter to them what color you were or what unrealistic social system was in place. Their young love was in bloom and so was their mischievousness.

Dad was always the instigator as he was used to fighting his way toward proving a point. It was common for Black people to add a little flame to the fire by throwing popcorn off the balcony onto the White people who sat below. As they sat on the balcony, Dad talked Mom into throwing popcorn down over the balcony into the crowd below. Mom was so smitten with Dad she would have done just about anything for him. So here she was being mischievous and radical, but in the back of her mind, she knew these actions would come back to bite her. Dad, on the other hand, was almost comfortable with walking on the wild side. It was nothing new for him to rebel against either White or Black people. He felt he was not accepted by either side, so whenever an opportunity presented him with a chance to stoke the fire, he would.

It never was made clear to me what movie they were watching, and I can only imagine between the make-out sessions and all the popcorn throwing that was going on, I'm not sure if anyone in the movie was really paying attention to the big screen.

Several days later, Mom realized the still small voice she heard warning her about this sudden defiant behavior of throwing popcorn on strangers was going to come back to haunt her. She reasoned it was just noise in her head. She had gotten so caught up in the moment that she forgot the theater was one of the buildings her mother worked at cleaning the bathrooms. It just so happened the usher working in the theater that day also cleaned bathrooms and had recognized Mom and reported his findings to my grandmother. As soon as my grandmother digested all this information, she quickly gave my mother an extended punishment with the worst stipulation my mother could have ever imagined: she was not to see my dad again.

As fate would have it, Dad ran into Mom again one day while walking near her home. She tried to avoid eye contact, but he knew she was deliberately trying to avoid him. Not willing to give in easily, Dad ignored the deliberate attempt to avoid him when she suddenly screamed out, "Mother says I can't see you anymore!" That was a phrase that Dad had often heard before, but he was determined that she would not have the last say in this situation. He quickly grabbed Mom's arm and swung her around when he noticed she was crying. It took a little bit of persuading, but after a while, Mom told him about the man from the theater who saw her throwing popcorn and shared that story with her mother which lead to her punishment. Dad was very consoling and vowed to make everything right again.

Dad knew he had to face the fact he had been the instigator in that popcorn throwing scenario, and he needed to tell her mother that if anyone should be punished, it should be him. He resolved to accomplish this mission the next day.

As Dad arrived at Mom's home the next day, he could not deny the pit of fear and doubt he felt in his stomach. After all, Mom had warned him her mother had low tolerance for any shenanigans. He also started to feel nervous about the fact she kept a gun under her bed mattress. Flashbacks of his evil Uncle Fred's knife attack on him tried to invade his thinking, but Dad was so determined to make this wrong a right that he ignored his fear and doubt and knocked on the door.

To his surprise, my grandmother opened the door and stood aside as he walked through the door. She asked him to come into the living room for a talk. He noticed that Mom was nowhere around. Her mother's face looked stern and authoritative again, but he sensed something a little different this time. Still, Dad made every effort to be cautious in how he presented his side of the story to her.

After sharing his side of the story, Dad learned something new about the character of my grandmother. She had explained to him the life she had led as a young pregnant wife on a cotton farm in the South. She went on to explain that a few years later, her husband had been killed in a car accident and how his family had rejected her and my mom, leaving them to survive on their own. She pointed out that it was only through God's grace and a few of her friends and family members that they eventually moved and started a life of their own.

From that day on, my dad and grandmother developed a loving mutual respect for each other that lasted over both their lives. I often heard my grandmother say she would cut anyone that messed with her son-in-law. Somehow, we all knew she meant every word of that—even though she was only about four feet nine in stature—we never questioned her ability to accomplish it. But me and Dad joked about where in the world she kept her knife!

A couple of years later, my parents were married in a courthouse ceremony which consisted of my parents, my grandmother and me! My mom wanted to complete her senior year of high school before getting married, but due to her pregnancy, my grandmother did not approve of that plan. Jokingly, Dad always told me he did not want to chance finding out my grandmother might also have a shotgun hidden somewhere, so they moved the date up and started their life together on May 29, 1954, in a quaint little courthouse ceremony.

Early in their marriage, my parents moved in with my grandmother, but my dad liked his independence and soon found his newfound family an apartment in a housing project about twenty miles away. The housing project was newly constructed with two bedrooms, a living room, a kitchen, and a bathroom. It served our family well for about three years, but Dad never really approved of the tenants that hung around some of the apartments.

He always said that he loved the beauty and nature of a wide-open tract of land. As soon as he worked to save enough money, he brought some land further out in a rural section. He had just enough money remaining to buy a small trailer he placed on the land for us to live in. The trailer resembled a cute little bungalow, and Dad even built a porch on to the front which gave it nice curb appeal. The land was adjacent to a farm with lots of farm animals. There were mornings we were awakened by the crow of a rooster and, on a hot summer day, suffered through smelling the stench of a group of hogs.

Dad loved nature and being free to live around the inhabitants of nature. The tract of land he brought was in the middle of nowhere. There were no modern conveniences like paved roads or streetlights. The roads were dusty, and after the sun went down, the area turned pitch-black. It was a blank canvas to Dad. He could add to or rearrange anything he wanted without being under rules and regulations from a third party.

Mom, on the other hand, learned to adapt to this new life of living adventurously raw in nature by taking one day at a time. Some days were not as good as others. For instance, one day she was playing with me in the front yard. Summer days were very hot and humid, so she liked to put me in a small rubber pool to splash around in the water. While I splashed around in the pool, she decided to walk to the mailbox, which was only a few feet down the driveway.

Out of the corner of her eye, she saw a large mother hog and two of her babies approaching me in my little rubber pool. Without even thinking, she flew into "mother attack mode," and walked right up to that mother hog kicking and screaming. The mother hog and her babies apparently only wanted a drink from the nice cool water they saw in my baby pool but were quickly shooed away by all the karate kicks and the ninja warrior stance my mother had quickly taken up.

Dad received a tongue lashing that day from Mom about moving the family to such a rural and uncivilized place to live. It did not matter to Dad that Mom was aggravated about the incident that had just taken place with the hogs. He was a visionary and could not let go of the vision and purpose he had to purchase real estate. He told me years later he had envisioned buying tracts of land all around the area. His disapproval of some of the rowdy tenants who lived in the housing projects motivated him to move his family away from that environment. He made a vow to himself that his family would never live there again. So, after calming Mom down that day, he assured her he would speak to the owner of the hogs about the incident.

The next day, he promptly went to talk to the owner of the hogs, but in a strange twist, he decided to forget it and instead talked about purchasing tracts of land. The owner's home was a farm by day, but at night, it quickly turned into the friendly Do Drop Inn, which became the neighborhood juke joint. During evening hours and all during the night, folks came from all around to drink moonshine liquor, sing, dance, story tell, and play cards. Dad was no stranger to this type of environment as it reminded him of the days he spent cleaning liquor bottles on Bill's boat.

He was determined to make a deal the owner could not refuse, so he came back later that night and challenged him to a game of cards with the result being he would pay a meager amount to purchase several tracts of land. During his time traveling with the circus sideshow as a barker, he learned the skill of storytelling. I remember growing up listening to some of his stories. Most of them were mysterious and adventurous but comical. The stories humorously captivated your attention to the point you could not tell the difference between truth and fantasy. That night, Dad won the card game and must have really told a whopper of a story because he made the deal of the century by obtaining the land.

The next few years—with the grace of God—Dad went from working as a custodian at the hospital to working with a construction company where he excelled in learning building techniques. He remembered as a kid watching his Grandpa Henry make things with his hands from pieces and scrapes of wood. That creative process had always amazed him. Now, years later, he lovingly reminisced over the techniques his grandpa had taught him about making things and readily applied them to home DIY projects.

The biggest project of them all was building the next house his growing family was going to live in. The little bungalow trailer my parents and I lived in sufficed for a while, but with the arrival of my other siblings, Dad knew he had to expand our homestead, and he did that. Over his lifetime, he built our family four houses from bits and pieces of scraps of building material he accumulated from working construction. The fact that my family never paid a mortgage for any of the homes we lived in attests to the goodness of the Lord and how God's grace and mercy covered Dad's life and livelihood.

The last house he built, which is presently where my mom lives today, will always be a source of fond memories for me. During the time Dad was building that house, I had doubted what God was doing through him. I did not have the faith that Dad would ever be able to complete building the house. I placed limitations on Dad's ability to accomplish what he believed he could do because of his circumstances. Unknowingly, I placed faithless expectations on Dad's ability to follow through with this house-building project. I should have known better than to doubt because I had watched Dad struggle with insecurity, low self-worth, and self-esteem issues most of my life only to see how he overcame them triumphantly each time. That same lack of faith reminds me of what Jesus told his disciples in Matthew 17:20 (NLT): "You don't have enough faith . . . I tell you the truth, if you had faith even as small as a mustard seed, you could say to this mountain, 'move from here to there,' and it would move. Nothing would be impossible."

Eventually, the empty mudholes and mounds of red clay dirt slowly evolved into a four-bedroom, two-car garage, all brick basement rancher home for our family. Needless to say, I learned a thing or two about faith by watching Dad plow tirelessly into building our family homestead. It took a while to accomplish the goal, but he never gave up. That raw determination I saw in him coupled with the many blessings God gifted to him will stay nestled in my heart and memory always.

CHAPTER 11: THE Departure

January 28, 2017

"Though my mother and father forsake me, the Lord will receive me." — Psalm 27:10 (NIV)

I T WAS A TYPICAL Saturday morning. I had gotten up to shower and perform my basic five steps to cover my wrinkles with makeup when my phone rang. When I answered, the only thing I could hear was a muffling sound but then the loud piercing sound of my mother's screams. There were loud sounds of desperation and fear calling out for help. My legs almost gave out from under me when my younger brother's voice finally yelled out, "Dad's had a heart attack!" From that point on, I was in an out-of-body experience. It's strange that your mind can go into autopilot. I somehow arrived at my parent's home, but I don't even remember driving there.

Much of that day seemed like a blur of time to me now. The ambulance had taken him to the hospital specializing in trauma and heart conditions. As I walked into the bedroom, I saw my mother slumped over a chair still crying loudly. She had been so hysterical and probably suffered from some trauma watching the paramedics attend to my dad. I was really concerned for her mental status at that point. She was completely broken. My dad had been her source of stability and security during their marriage of sixty-three years.

Even though I felt my senior years would bring me wisdom and strength upon entering the hospital that day, I really had to pray for my faith and courage to sustain me. I had not been in a hospital setting since I was fifty-nine when my husband passed three years prior. As the double doors opened and I walked into the lobby, the standard decor and even the smell were all coming back to me. During my husband's illness from gastric cancer, I spent a long time taking care of him in the hospital. Now the reality of what was currently happening was starting to make me feel weak and nauseous. I could not believe this was happening to me again. The feeling of not having control—panic and fear set in. It was too much to bear.

I searched for the nearest ladies' room to duck inside before the tears started rolling down my face. My emotions had reached a point of no return. I couldn't stop what was happening to me, so I just gave in to it. Luckily, the bathroom only accommodated one person. It seemed the area was just enough space to catch me as I fell into despair. How could this happen? Why did this happen?

My dad was my hero. We could talk and discuss anything. He always made me feel so special. I could always depend on him . . . especially now since my husband was gone. I felt so alone.

I don't remember leaving that bathroom or even walking down the long hallway to the ICU unit. The only thing I am sure about is I had no physical strength that day. God supplied power that day because I had no strength to keep me vertical. It was all through God's grace and mercy.

As I entered the ICU where my dad was located, my eyes were drawn to all the different kinds of life-saving equipment and machines placed around the area. Dad looked disheveled and uncomfortable lying in the bed. His eyes were open and seem to follow me as I walked closer. I grabbed his huge hand. It was a standing joke between us that his hands were that big just to scare away anyone he thought might mean harm to anyone in our family.

For a moment, he seemed to try to say something, but his eyes told me this was a struggle.

As I stood in that room watching the medical personnel care for my dad, I felt a numbness come over me. My mind wandered to the numerous times he and I shared funny jokes and discussed obstacles about his life and learning experiences. We made a promise to love one another even in situations where we had a difference of opinion. We vowed to always love each other no matter what happened.

A sense of disbelief began to pierce me. I did not want to accept the reality of what was happening at this moment. I wanted to run away from that room and scream as loud as I could, but then this sense of unnatural calm slipped under my feet. I remember trying to resist at first, but its pull was convincing enough that I surrendered to its strength.

In the week that followed, my dad's condition slowly deteriorated. My brothers and sister-in-law all took turns to stay with him. One day, I noticed he kept looking up toward the ceiling. It was as if he was following something moving around the room. It was a subtle gesture at first, but as the days moved forward, his stare became more intense, and he started to lift his arms.

The next few days were an emotional rollercoaster that I could not believe I was riding daily. At first, Dad seemed to be cognitive of his surroundings, but as time passed, he began to drift in and out of a comatose state. The first day he slowly began to raise his hands, I did not think much of it, but each day as my sister-in-law and I visited him, he would start to raise his hands until his physical strength could not sustain it. I no longer believed this gesture was subtle but an indication that angels were placed around his room.

My sister-in-law and I were both witness to this supernatural presence, so we positioned ourselves on each side of him and helped him lift his hands. I remembered his favorite gospel song was the song from the movie, *The Color Purple*. I quietly began to sing the chorus to the song, "God's Trying to Tell You Something." The song centered around a wayward daughter returning to a father who needed to forgive her. Every time Dad heard this song, I knew he was touched. Looking back on the events of his life, I started to feel an empty throbbing feeling in the pit of my stomach.

I knew my dad was leaving this place for a better place. That final week as I sat at my dad's bedside, I believe I witnessed the beginning of his transition from this life here on Earth to his eternal life with the Lord. For several days, Dad lay between a comatose and delirious state. His eyes were constantly fixed on the ceiling above him.

I was in complete denial that any of this was unfolding while false optimism slipped into my thinking. I suppose part of being in denial is the trickery behind the thought. I began to think that Dad would soon be up and about, telling his funny jokes and stories and working like he always did when times got hard. When it came to his work ethic, I knew all too well about his great physical strength. Heck, I once saw him pick up an entire refrigerator and place it in the back of his truck, but I also was aware of the status of his mental strength over his last months of life, and I knew he was becoming weary.

At that moment I did not want to think of letting him go, so I began to pray and ask the Lord to sustain me with strength and peace to help me not succumb to the distress I was beginning to feel. As I look back at that desperate moment, I am reminded of a verse from the Bible that has served as a guiding light to me. Isaiah 40:31 (NIV) says, "but those who hope in the Lord will renew their strength. They will soar on wings like eagles; they will run and not grow weary, they will walk and not be faint."

The following morning, my sweet Daddy went home to be with the Lord. A sense of numbness crept into my soul and impacted my routine the next couple of days. My dad had been my provider and my protector, the person that would always be there for me when I needed help. Now just like that, he was gone.

I wanted to run somewhere and pretend that none of it was true. My mind was racing, and after a while of struggling with unbridled distraught feelings, I found solace in running to a secret place I could cry out to the Lord, which happened to be my car. I must have sobbed uncontrollably for what seemed like hours, but at the end of trying to process my emotions, I started to feel the peace and strength that I had previously prayed for in Dad's hospital room. Even to this day, I still thank the Lord for providing me with what I needed to function and get through that difficult time of loss.

My family, especially my mother, was in a state of lifeless shock after that. Dad's passing was especially hard for her. He was everything to her, and I was concerned for her mental health. After all, Mom had been his wife through young adulthood, middle age, and now walking in the reality of loss in her senior years. My siblings and I were all living with the hurt and pain that comes when a parent dies, but at the same time, we knew we had the love and support of each other. Most importantly, we had our precious memories of Dad and everything he stood for and had worked so hard to accomplish. That fact alone was what we all clung to for survival during the days that followed.

The funeral service preparation was one of the hardest things that our family had ever walked through. Planning for his service was emotional and heart-wrenching for me. Mom was struggling to cope with all the trauma she had witnessed during the past few days. My heart was hurting for her, and at the same time, hurting for myself too. I resolved to be stronger to cover the hurt for both of us. The funeral director I previously used to handle my husband's service three years prior was very accommodating, and I was so thankful for the assistance they continued to give me. But I was having trouble keeping myself from falling apart.

I simply could not wrap my mind around the finality that my dad was no longer around. I was beginning to feel the pain of loss of not only him being around to talk and laugh with but also to fix things for me or have those heated debate discussions we would have that seemed to always end in a round of laughter.

As preparations for the funeral service continued, the question came up about who would deliver the eulogy. Every name that was suggested was quickly eliminated. I knew deep down in my heart no one could deliver this personal story like I could. Dad had never been someone who attended church on a weekly basis. As a matter of fact, he told funny stories about the few times as an adult that he did attend and how it was either because someone was getting married or buried.

Strangely enough, he pointed out to me how important it was to him as a youth that Virgie took him to church. I knew there was also a root of social and religious hurt the church he attended as a youth allowed to happen either through ignorance or White privilege or maybe both. Unfortunately, I believe our society clings to those same unfair, self-centered, power-hungry truths even in our current time. Trying to understand how emotionally hard those days must have been for him reminds me of the words found in Psalms 27:10 (NIV), "Though my father and mother forsake me, the Lord will receive me."

I could not believe the strength the Lord gave me on the day of Dad's funeral service. I was given that same victorious and supernatural strength a few years earlier at my husband's funeral service. As I now reminisce, I should not have been so surprised that if God allowed me to be an overcomer once, he would allow me to be an overcomer twice. As things would have it, I needed extra strength and power that day as the evil powers and principalities were determined to take me down with obstacles and situations that I'm convinced were being fought in the heavenly realm.

As I delivered the eulogy at Dad's funeral service, I delighted in the words spoken in Psalms 27:4–6 (NIV), "One thing I ask from the Lord, this only do I seek: that I may dwell in the house of the Lord all the days of my life, to gaze on the beauty of the Lord and to seek him in his temple. For in the day of trouble he will keep me safe in his dwelling; he will hide me in the shelter of his sacred tent and set me high upon a rock. Then my head will be exalted above the enemies who surround me; at his sacred tent I will sacrifice with shouts of joy; I will sing and make music to the Lord." A feeling of joy had taken residence in my heart with this proclamation found in God's Word because it stands as a consoling confirmation that Dad was ushered into the loving presence of our Lord and Savior Jesus Christ.

Joyously, I can say, "Yes! I take delight in the Lord!" This happened for me when I surrendered my heart and mind to his lordship. I now realize my desire is to surrender to the desire Jesus has for me in his divine will.

If you have read this book to this point, please know Jesus will keep his promise to give you perfect peace in a world filled with hurt and brokenness. Hold on to his hand, but more than anything, seek his face. Proverbs 3:7 tells me to not be wise in my own eyes but fear the Lord and turn away from evil. I understand this concept to be the very foundation of my saved life and the growth of my relationship with Jesus. If he did it for my dad and me, he can *surely* do it for you!

To God be the glory!

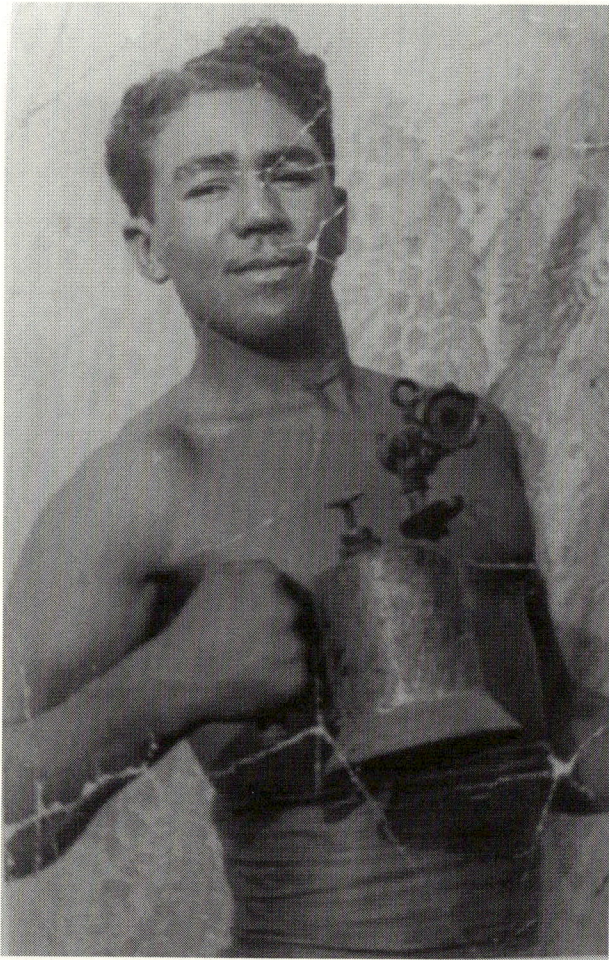

Fire Eater

In memoriam

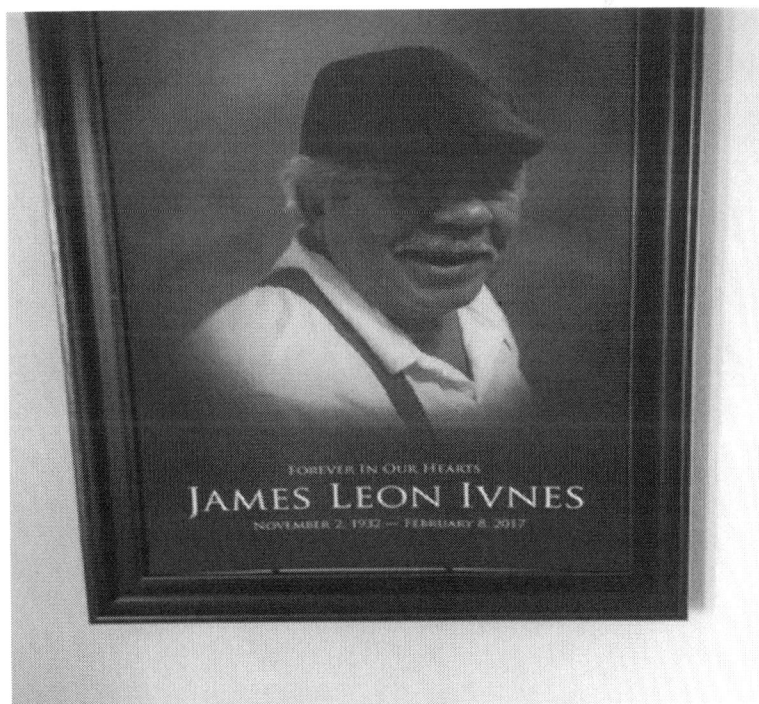

FOREVER IN OUR HEARTS

JAMES LEON IVNES

NOVEMBER 2, 1932 — FEBRUARY 8, 2017

Afterword

More than ever, the times we are currently living in certainly require mankind to surrender from being self-centered, money-hungry, power-driven, unforgiving, non-compassionate individuals and start embracing a spirit of peaceful reconciliation and genuine forgiveness toward each other regardless of race, creed, or color. This is clearly illustrated in Revelation 7:9 (NIV) when it states, "After this I looked, and there before me was a great multitude that no one could count, from every nation, tribe, people and language, standing before the throne and before the Lamb." The work of reconciliation will flow when we turn our hearts to humbly listen to each other and open our eyes to see God's image in one another.

In a recent sermon I heard at my church, Overcoming Believers Church, my pastor quoted the words in Galatians 5:22–23 (NLT), "But the Holy Spirit produces this kind of fruit in our lives: love, joy, peace, patience, kindness, goodness, faithfulness, gentleness, and self-control. There is no law against these things!"

The fruit referenced in this chapter of Galatians as pointed out in the sermon can only be birthed out of practicing patience. As humans, we all have fallen short from times of being impatient, but we must not expect a fruitful life without sowing a spiritual seed in our spirit that takes root when we exercise the discipline of patience. Living through blatant racism and unequal civil rights was not easy for my father, but learning to not allow hate to constrain purpose and productivity in your life requires the fruit of patience. Martin Luther King Jr. once said, "Darkness cannot drive out darkness; only light can do that. Hate cannot drive out hate, only love can do that!"

Thank you, Daddy, for leaving me your legacy of love!
Octavia Yvonne Webb, 2021

ACKNOWLEDGMENTS

I want to thank Sherri Lavon Williams, CEO of Sols Write House Publishing, for her energetic inspiration to be an overcomer of personal tragedy and for her generosity to provide me with the resources I needed to get started to write this book.

I also want to thank Linda L. Smith- NITT Tech Services for the godly mentorship she provided to me, which resulted in bringing clarity to me that I can only write one book at a time during my draft writing experience.

A good friend who shared her book writing notes with me-Desiree I. Bowers, Author.

I also extend a thank you to my spiritual leaders and pastors of Overcoming Believers Church Pastor Daryl Arnold and First Lady Carmeisha Arnold for providing the spiritual guidance I needed in a special season of life.

I cannot go any further without thanking all the folks at Self-Publishing School: Joris, founder of Cutting Edge Studios; Carly Catt of Catt Editing; and especially Kerk Murray, my personal writing coach. His interpersonal skills are unmatched, and even though I haven't known him that long, I feel like he has been not only my coach but my friend for years.

I also send out a loving thank you to my beautiful mother and my family who stand by me and scratch their heads wondering what I will be doing next. I do these things because I love you all!

In closing, I want to thank my Lord and Savior Jesus Christ for never leaving me and carrying me on the many days I wanted to give up on this project. You are my everything! AMEN!

ABOUT THE AUTHOR

Octavia Yvonne Webb is retired and lives in Knoxville, Tennessee. Her greatest loves are her faith in Jesus Christ and her family, especially her five grandchildren. She is currently a Bible study teacher at Serenity House, a rehabilitative women's shelter. She attends Overcoming Believers Church where she serves as a coordinator for Love Thy Neighbor Food Ministry.

Made in the USA
Middletown, DE
30 December 2021

57185682R00057